The Justin Wilson #2 Cookbook: Cookin' Cajun

The Justin Wilson #2 Cookbook: Cookin' Cajun

by

Justin Wilson

PELICAN PUBLISHING
NEW ORLEANS

First printing, 1979
Second printing, 1982
Third printing, 1984
Fourth printing, 1985
Fifth printing, 1986
Sixth printing, 1986
Seventh printing, 1986
Eighth printing, 1987
Ninth printing, 1988
Tenth printing, 1990
Eleventh printing, 1991
Twelfth printing, 1994
Thirteenth printing, 2000
Fourteenth printing, 2006
Fifteenth printing, 2009
Sixteenth printing, 2012
Seventeenth printing, 2014
Eighteenth printing, 2022

Library of Congress Cataloging in Publication Data

Wilson, Justin
The Justin Wilson No. 2 cookbook, Cookin' Cajun

1. Cookery, American—Louisiana. 2. Cookery, Creole. I. Title. II. Title: Cookin' Cajun.
TX715.W7493 641.5'9763 79-20571
ISBN 9781455627448

Printed in the United States of America
Published by Pelican Publishing
New Orleans, LA
www.pelicanpub.com

Designed by Mike Burton

To ma wife, Sara, and all ma wonderful Cajun friens' who helped me make dis book possible.

Foreword

Dese recipes in dis book may not be what some people in South Louisiana would call Cajun. Dey are, howsomeever, Cajun 'cause the main Cajun ingredients are in dem. Dat is, seasoning, fun, imagination, and common sense. It has been and is a pleasure to cook as I do wit' help an' a lot of advice from people mentioned in ma dedication. Cook from dis book an' have your enjoys all the way plumb. You will, I garontee!

Contents

How to Make a Roux

The roux is the foundation of many, many Cajun dishes. You will find it referred to in a number of the recipes in this book.

The roux which follows is the one I have used for many years with great success. I garontee!

Roux

1½ cups sifted flour
olive oil

Cover the bottom of a heavy pot with olive oil. After the olive oil is well heated over a low fire, add the flour. Cook the flour very slowly, stirring almost constantly. (Cook for about 45 minutes.) The flour must be browned to a very dark brown, nearly black, but not actually burned.

This takes more time than you might think is necessary, but a good roux must be cooked slowly to get all the floury taste out of it and to insure uniformity of color.

Although all roux are pretty much the same in Cajun kitchens, there are variations practiced by some stubborn ol' cooks which I won't attempt to go into here.

However, as you read this book, you'll see where several recipes call for a couple of additional ingredients.

For instance, after you have made the basic roux, you may be instructed to add a small can of tomato paste, stirring this constantly until the roux has reached the color of the flour before the paste was added. Then add a small can of tomato sauce, stirring this into the mixture until it all turns dark brown again. This is only one of the many variations of the basic roux.

Appetizers and Dips

Copper Pennies

SAUCE:
½ cup salad oil
1 cup sugar
¾ cup vinegar
1 can tomato soup
1 tbsp. powdered mustard
1 tbsp. Worcestershire
2 lbs. carrots, sliced
1 medium onion, sliced
1 small green pepper, sliced

Simmer in a saucepan the salad oil, sugar, vinegar, tomato soup, mustard, and Worcestershire sauce.

Boil the carrots until tender. (Remember, if you use canned carrots, you don't have to cook them!) In a casserole dish, alternate in layers the carrots, onions, and peppers. Pour sauce over the vegetables and refrigerate.

Le' me tol' you the wondermous part about us Cajuns. We don't need no appetizers 'cause we got an appetite soon as we sit down, yeah. I don' even need no cookin' aromas, no. The kind of appetite I got wake up wit' me in the mornin', every mornin'. I tol' you for true!

Shrimp Dip

1 can tomato soup
½ cup catsup
4 tsp. Louisiana hot sauce (or 2 tsp. Tabasco)
½ tsp. onion juice
¼ tsp. garlic salt
½ tsp. minced celery
dash of paprika
dash of cayenne pepper
2 tbsp. creamed butter

Combine all of the ingredients, except butter, and whip together well. Chill. Just before serving, blend in the butter until the mixture becomes smooth. Use for dunking shrimp.

Dis is me an' ma good frien', Les Brown. An' I wanna tol' you, he is a good crawfish people. He caught dem crawfish for me an' he loves to did dat.

Crawfish Cocktail

20 to 25 lbs. crawfish

SAUCE:
½ cup chili sauce
½ cup catsup
¼ cup horseradish
1½ tsp. Worcestershire
¼ tsp. salt
2 tsp. lemon juice
½ cup finely minced celery
Tabasco (or cayenne pepper sauce)

Boil the crawfish in well-salted water about 15 minutes. Mix the rest of the ingredients together for the cocktail sauce.

Fill a large bowl with chopped ice and arrange crawfish tails over the top. Provide toothpicks for handy dipping. Serve with cocktail sauce.

Party Cheese Ball

2 pkg. (8 oz. each) cream cheese
1 pkg. (8 oz.) cheddar cheese, shredded
1 tbsp. chopped pimento
1 tbsp. chopped green pepper
1 tbsp. finely chopped onion
1 tsp. fresh lemon juice
2 tsp. Worcestershire
dash of cayenne pepper (or Louisiana hot sauce)
dash of salt
pecans, finely chopped

Blend together the cream cheese and shredded cheddar cheese. Add all of the other ingredients except the pecans; mix well.

Shape into a ball and roll in chopped pecans. Wrap, and chill for 24 hours in the refrigerator. Serve with crackers or chips. Makes one 1½-pound cheese ball.

Tabasco Marinated Shrimp

- 3 lbs. raw shrimp (fresh or frozen)
- 2 12-oz. bottles (or cans) beer
- ½ tsp. Tabasco sauce
- 1 tbsp. salt
- 1 tbsp. dry mustard
- 2 tbsp. vinegar
- 1 slice onion
- 2 tbsp. honey
- ¼ tsp. bitters (Peychaud or Angostura)

Remove shells and veins from shrimp. Rinse. In a saucepan, combine beer, Tabasco, salt, mustard, vinegar, onion, honey, and bitters. Bring to a boil and simmer about 1 minute. Add only enough cleaned shrimp as will be covered by the liquid mixture; return the mixture to a boil and then simmer 2 to 5 minutes, depending on the size of the shrimp. Remove shrimp from the liquid, add remaining shrimp, and repeat the cooking procedure.

Cool both the shrimp and the liquid. Return the shrimp to the cooled liquid and marinate for several hours. Drain.

Serve with wooden picks as hors d'oeuvres or an appetizer. Makes approximately 2 dozen servings.

Tangy Meatballs

- 1 lb. ground beef
- 1 egg, slightly beaten
- ¼ cup chili sauce
- ¼ cup finely chopped onion
- 1 tsp. salt
- ¼ tsp. ground red pepper
- 1½ cups cheese cracker crumbs
- cooking oil

Combine the ground beef, egg, chili sauce, chopped onion, salt, and pepper with 1 cup cheese cracker crumbs. Mix thoroughly. Shape into tiny meatballs and roll in the remaining ½ cup cracker crumbs.

Sauté the meatballs 5 minutes in ½ inch hot cooking oil, turning to brown on all sides. Remove to a chafing dish and serve with toothpicks. Makes about thirty meatballs.

Soups and Salads

Rice Salad

- 2 cups rice
- 1 cup chopped green onion
- 1 cup chopped dill pickle
- 1 cup chopped sweet pickle
- 1 cup chopped celery
- 1 cup chopped bell pepper
- 1 cup chopped olives (with pimento)
- 1 cup salad dressing
- 1½ cups finely chopped hard-boiled egg
- 3 to 4 tbsp. Durkee's sauce
- 3 tbsp. prepared yellow mustard
- cayenne pepper to taste
- olive oil
- 3 dashes wine vinegar

Cook the rice according to the directions on the package. Combine in a bowl the onion, pickles, celery, bell pepper, olives, egg, and cooked rice.

Mix together thoroughly the salad dressing, Durkee's, mustard, cayenne pepper, olive oil, and wine vinegar. Blend in with the dry ingredients. Refrigerate the whole darn mess.

By the way, this is better if refrigerated and served the next day.

Chili I

- 4 lbs. chili meat, ground coarsely or cut in small pieces
- 2 tbsp. chili powder
- 2 tbsp. Hershey's cocoa
- 2 cups chopped onion
- 1 cup chopped bell pepper
- garlic, chopped
- Louisiana hot sauce
- salt
- 1 6-pack beer
- bacon drippings (or olive oil)

Brown the meat off in bacon drippings or olive oil. Add the beer, chili powder, cocoa, and other ingredients. Let cook at least an hour. An' its better if you let it cook slowly for 3 hours.

It's delicious! And you can't taste the cocoa!

Chili II

- 4 lbs. chili meat, ground coarsely or cut in small pieces
- 2 tbsp. chili powder
- 4 cups sauterne wine
- 4 cups water
- 2 tbsp. Hershey's cocoa
- 2 cups chopped onion
- 1 cup chopped bell pepper
- garlic, chopped
- Louisiana hot sauce
- salt
- bacon drippings (or olive oil)

Brown the meat off in bacon drippings or olive oil. Add the wine and water. Add the rest of the ingredients and let cook for at least an hour. Again, it's better if you cook for 3 hours.

Seafood Gumbo

- 2 cups olive oil
- 5 cups flour
- 6 cups onions
- 3 cups chopped bell pepper
- 2 cups chopped green onion
- 2 cans (8 oz. each) tomato sauce
- ½ cup garlic
- 1½ cups finely chopped parsley
- 2 cups sauterne wine
- 2 doz. crabs
- 3 lbs. shrimp, peeled and deveined
- 4 tbsp. Lea & Perrins
- 2 tsp. cayenne pepper
- 6 qts. water
- 3 tbsp. salt (But this may not be enough or may be too much. Taste first, then add.)
- filé

Make a very dark roux. (See my recipe.) Add the onions and bell pepper, stirring constantly until the onions become clear. Pour in the tomato sauce and green onion, and cook until the roux is back to its original dark color. Add garlic, parsley, water, Lea & Perrins, salt, cayenne pepper, and wine.

Cook the mixture for 45 minutes, then drop in the crabs and shrimp. (Clean the crabs first by placing them in boiling water. Use only the bodies, broken in half, and the large claws.) Let cook for two or more hours.

Filé does not go in the pot! When you're ready to eat, sprinkle the filé over the rice and cover with steaming hot gumbo.

Oyster Chowder

1 cup diced Irish potatoes
2 tbsp. olive oil
1 cup chopped celery
1 cup chopped onion
½ cup chopped parsley
1 tsp. Louisiana hot sauce (or ½ tsp. Tabasco)
1 tsp. chopped garlic
3 cups juice from oysters (with water added if necessary)
1 cup sauterne wine
1 tbsp. soy sauce
2 tsp. salt
2 cups oysters

Cook the potatoes until tender. Sauté celery, onion, and parsley in olive oil until clear or nearly done. Add garlic. Add the oyster juice and wine to the sautéed vegetables.

Add the potatoes with the water they are in. Bring to a boil, then cut down to a low simmer (about 170° to 175°). Add the oysters, salt, soy sauce, and Louisiana hot sauce.

Let the whole thing simmer for at least 6 hours, or even better, let simmer overnight.

Scallop Chowder

6 tbsp. butter (or margarine)
2 shallots, diced
1 leaf celery, diced
2 onions, diced
1½ lbs. peeled, washed, and diced potatoes
1 tbsp. salt
2½ cups water
1 lb. scallops
1 pt. whipping cream
1 tbsp. chopped parsley
pepper
1 cup sauterne wine

Sauté the celery and onions slowly in melted butter until the onions are transparent. Add shallots. Blend in potatoes, salt, pepper, sauterne, and water. Bring to a boil, and add scallops and their juice, if any. Bring back to a boil, then cut the heat and cook for 10 minutes.

Heat the whipping cream to a boiling point in a separate pan. Stir it into the chowder along with the parsley and a little more salt (if needed).

Makes ten to twelve servings.

Some time when the weather is real bad it's best to use a silver hook to caught dem fish like I'm doin' rat now, instead of goin' out dare an' tryin' to caught dem in the river. An' I know dat ol' Murphy is not goin' to sold me some fish dat are not so good, no.

Lobster Salad

- 4 cups cooked lobster (or crawfish)
- 3 hard-boiled eggs, chopped
- ½ cup celery
- ¼ cup chopped green onion
- 2 crisp apples, peeled, cored, and diced
- 1 banana, sliced
- mayonnaise
- ¼ cup sour cream

Toss together lightly (so as not to mash) everything except the mayonnaise and sour cream. Add the mayonnaise, lightened with ¼ cup sour cream. Serve with banana bread or plantain chips.

Chicken Gumbo

- 1 large onion, chopped fine
- 1 large clove garlic, chopped fine
- 4 cups sauterne wine
- 4 cups water
- 2 tbsp. Worcestershire
- 1 2-lb. chicken, cut up
- 1 fresh hot pepper (or 1 tsp. Louisiana hot sauce or ½ tsp. Tabasco)
- 1 lb. andouille sausage, in ¼-in. slices
- salt to taste

First you make a roux. (See my recipe.) Add all of the ingredients to the roux and simmer until the chicken and sausage are done. It's *some* good, I garontee!

The trouble wit' people is dey don' know what andouille sausage is. It's sausage used for makin' gumbo, like dis chicken gumbo. Or use it wit' rice or Irish potatoes. It's damn good eatin' sausage wit' anyt'ing. A pine burr taste good wit' andouille. Dare ain't no question about dat, no!

Seafood Soup

- 3 cups raw fish, boned and cubed
- 1 cup chopped celery
- 1 white and 1 green onion, chopped
- 1 cup chopped bell pepper
- 1 cup cubed carrots
- 1 lime, chopped
- 1 clove garlic, chopped fine
- 2 tbsp. dried parsley (or 1 cup fresh)
- 2 cups crawfish, shrimp, crabmeat, or oysters
- ½ tsp. cayenne pepper
- salt to taste

Combine all of the vegetables and cover with about 1 inch water. Boil until tender. Add the fish and crawfish; boil with the seasoning until cooked well. (Shrimp, crabmeat, or oysters may be used instead of crawfish.)

I think it's a good idea to boil the soup for approximately 30 minutes, then simmer for 1½ hours. Then you will got you some fine tastin' soup, I garontee!

Ooh boy! Dat's a relief, I garontee! It came out jus' like I t'ought it would. But I had my own doubts dare for a little while, you hear!

Avocado Soup

2 cups chopped avocado
1 tsp. salt
$1\frac{1}{2}$ cups chicken stock (or canned chicken broth)
1 tbsp. Worcestershire
dash of Louisiana hot sauce
2 cups buttermilk

Put all of the ingredients in a blender and liquefy. Refrigerate. Serve cold.

Nookie Diaz' Oyster Fisherman Soup

9 doz. oysters
2 lbs. salt meat
1 large black iron pot
onions
bell peppers
celery
garlic
parsley
flour
shell noodles
canned whole tomatoes
onion tops
Tabasco sauce
salt
pepper
Lea & Perrins
You

Use a big black iron pot. Chop 2 pounds salt meat in small hunks and boil for approximately 15 minutes. Drain the salt meat and fry until it is well browned. Take salt meat out, put a heaping tablespoon of flour into the grease, and brown. (If there is not enough fat, add oil.)

Add two big chopped onions. After they have cooked down somewhat, add $\frac{3}{4}$ of a small can of whole tomatoes and cook a little while. Add oyster water. (Use as much oyster water as you can get. If not enough, use water.) Put the salt meat back in, and add one-half of a bell pepper, three leaves of celery, and three cloves of garlic, all chopped.

Let cook for 45 minutes to an hour, checking occasionally to see that the water doesn't run out. Add the oysters and let cook for about 15 minutes. Season at this time with pepper, Lea & Perrins, Tabasco, and salt (if necessary).

Add one cup of shell noodles, onion tops, and parsley. Cook until the noodles are done (approximately 20 minutes). Serve in soup plates.

Seafood Gumbo with Okra

okra, cut
2 large onions, chopped fine
1 medium bell pepper, chopped fine
1 large clove garlic, chopped fine
4 cups sauterne wine
2 lbs. shrimp, shelled
1 pt. crabmeat
1 pt. drained oysters
4 cups water
1 tsp. Louisiana hot sauce (or ½ tsp. Tabasco)
2 tbsp. Worcestershire
4 tsp. salt
filé

First you make a roux. (Follow my recipe.) Sauté the okra separately. Add onion and bell pepper to the roux and cook until both are clear or soft. Add wine, garlic, and the rest of the ingredients. (You should never add garlic to anything until there is some juice or liquid.)

Cook over a low fire for 2 or more hours. When you serve, sprinkle some filé over the rice before putting gumbo over it.

Vegetable Soup

Get a good piece of soup meat, preferably a beef brisket with fat, because that's where the flavor is. Cover meat with water. See what you have in your pantry or your refrigerator to put in there, such as:

sliced carrots (We mean sliced crossedwise, not lengthwise, no.)
snap beans
turnips
potatoes
butter beans
English peas
whole grain corn
celery

Use any kind of vegetable you have! Add parsley, salt, and Louisiana hot sauce (or Tabasco) to taste. Bring to a boil. Let it simmer about 2 hours.

Sprinkle filé on top when you serve. (Filé is green sassafras leaves that are ground and dried. And will it add flavor. Ooh boy!)

Meats

Stuffed Peppers, Cajun Style

8 green bell peppers
1 cup yellow cornmeal
1½ lbs. ground lean beef
1 clove garlic, mashed
1 tbsp. chili powder
1 can (1-lb. can) kidney beans, well drained
1 egg, well beaten
1½ tsp. salt
1 tsp. cayenne pepper
1 cup minced onion
½ cup tomato sauce
¼ cup chopped pimento
½ cup dry bread crumbs
8 strips bacon
½ cup sauterne wine
½ cup water

Slice the tops from peppers and remove seeds. Cook cornmeal into a mush in the water and sauterne. (Add more water if necessary.) Spoon the mush into the peppers, spreading mush to line each. Combine the remaining ingredients, except bacon, blend well, and stuff into the peppers.

Place peppers side by side in a shallow pan, and top with bacon strips. Add water to the pan. Bake, uncovered, in a preheated moderate oven (325°). Cook for 1 hour, or until done. Serve hot.

Baked and Broiled Pork Chops

6 pork chops
salt
ground red cayenne pepper
1 tbsp. soy sauce
1 cup sauterne wine

Preheat oven to 350°. Grease pan.

Salt and red pepper the pork chops on both sides. Put in 350-degree oven for 10 minutes. Put oven on broil. Mix wine and soy sauce together and pour over the pork chops when they begin to brown.

Broil the pork chops until browned on both sides. Serves six.

Rat here, I'm fixin' to stuff dem garlic down in dare. I'm gonna put some other seasoning in dare, too. An' it is gonna be good. Ooh boy!

Turkey and Ham in the Smoker Cooker

- ham
- turkey
- 1 apple
- whole garlic cloves
- salt
- ground red cayenne pepper
- hot green peppers
- shallots
- ½ tsp. bitters (Peychaud or Angostura)
- 2 tbsp. Worcestershire
- 2 cups sauterne wine
- 2 onions
- 1 tbsp. liquid smoke

Cut the apple and one onion in half and stuff them in the turkey. Put a few whole garlic cloves in the turkey. Salt and pepper to taste.

Cut holes in the ham, and stuff each with garlic, pepper, and shallots. Do this in various places on both sides.

In the meantime, build the fire and get the charcoal going. Put hickory chips on the top. Place in the pan one onion, 2 cloves garlic, the bitters, liquid smoke, Worcestershire sauce, sauterne, and water. Put your turkey in the cooker first, and then the ham on top, so the fat from the ham will drip down and flavor the turkey.

Cook for 18 hours. Also, too, be sure you have water in the cooker at all times. If you don't, it will just dry out completely. Check the fire, too, because it may not last that long. Put the pan in there before you rekindle the fire, or the fire will go out. I've done it many a time, and it makes me so mad I couldn't spit.

Seven Steaks Etouffée

- 2 tbsp. cooking oil
- 7 steaks (or 1 round steak, making 4 lbs. total)
- 2 cans (6 oz. each) mushroom steak sauce
- 1 cup sauterne wine
- 1 cup chopped onion
- ¼ cup chopped pimento
- 2 tsp. chopped garlic
- 1 tsp. celery seed
- 1 tbsp. dried parsley
- 1 tbsp. soy sauce
- ¼ tbsp. bitters (Peychaud or Angostura)
- salt and pepper to taste
- 1 tsp. Louisiana hot sauce (or ½ tsp. Tabasco)

Heat the cooking oil in a Dutch oven. Add the meat, and cover with the rest of the ingredients. Salt and pepper to taste. Cover and let cook over low heat for 2 to 3 hours.

Cajunized Oriental Pork Chops

6 thick pork chops
salt and red pepper
1½ cups sauterne wine
1 cup chopped bell pepper
1 cup chopped onion
1 clove garlic, chopped
3 tbsp. soy sauce
1 can (15 oz.) pineapple chunks

Salt and red pepper the chops, and brown them slowly in a skillet. Add wine, bell pepper, onion, and garlic. Cover and simmer for 25 to 30 minutes. Remove pork chops, being sure to keep them warm.

Add the soy sauce and syrup from pineapple. Stir until more or less thick. Add the pineapple chunks and bring to a boil. Serve over pork chops and hot cooked rice. Makes six servings.

Glazed Ham Loaf

1½ lbs. lean fresh ground pork
1 lb. ground smoked ham
1 cup fine dry bread crumbs
1 tsp. salt
¾ tsp. prepared mustard
1 cup milk
2 eggs, well beaten
2 tbsp. finely chopped green pepper
½ cup brown sugar
½ cup water
¼ cup white vinegar
1 tbsp. dry mustard
½ cup sauterne wine

Blend pork, ham, bread crumbs, salt, prepared mustard, milk, eggs, and green pepper. (More green pepper may be added if desired.) Shape into a loaf; score the top in a diagonal crisscross pattern. Place in a well-greased, large shallow baking dish.

Combine the remaining ingredients in a small saucepan. Bring to a boil, stirring often. Pour the sauce over the loaf. Bake at 325° for 2 hours, basting occasionally. Serve the sauce over the loaf. Makes eight servings.

Corned Beef and Cabbage

3 to 5 lbs. corned beef
1 large cabbage
4 large whole onions
4 cups sauterne wine
2 tbsp. Worcestershire
1 whole cayenne pepper (or dash of Louisiana hot sauce)
salt

Cover corned beef with water. Add sauterne, Worcestershire, and cayenne pepper. Boil until tender (2 to 3 hours). Remove the corned beef. Cut the cabbage into quarters and add to the stock. Add whole onions, and boil until tender. Salt to taste.

Slice the corned beef and place over cabbage for each serving. Serves six to eight.

Backbone and Turnips

½ cup bacon drippings
3 cups chopped onion
3 to 4 lbs. pork backbone
1 cup bell pepper
1 cup celery
½ cup chopped parsley
1 tsp. chopped garlic
2 tsp. Worcestershire
ground red cayenne pepper
8 cups chopped turnips
3 tsp. salt
1 cup sauterne wine
water

First you make a roux. (Follow my recipe in the front of the book.)

Brown the backbone off in bacon drippings in a Dutch oven. Add onion, bell pepper, celery, and parsley to the roux. After you get some juice, add the garlic. Add the remaining ingredients, including the browned backbone, and pour enough water over it to cover. Cook 3 to 4 hours over medium heat.

Ma wife Sara and me, we agree. That's so good it oughta be against the law to make it more than once or twice a year!

What kinda wine to drink wit' dis fine food? Why, hell, the kind dat you likes the bes', dat's the kind.

Roast Pork With Applekraut

- 1 rolled pork loin roast, 2½ to 3 lbs.
- ½ tsp. garlic powder
- 1 tsp. cayenne pepper
- ½ cup butter (or margarine)
- 4 medium cooking apples, cored and sliced in rings
- 4 cups drained sauerkraut (2 16-oz. cans)
- ½ cup packed light brown sugar
- 1 tsp. dried mint
- 1 tsp. salt

Sprinkle meat with garlic powder, salt, pepper, and mint. Place the meat on the oven rack in an open roasting pan. Roast in 325-degree oven for 2 hours. Remove the roast from oven and let it stand 15 minutes for easier carving; remove strings.

Meanwhile, melt the butter in a large skillet. Add the apple rings, a few at a time, and cook until well browned. Stir in the remaining ingredients. Cover and cook over low heat 30 minutes, stirring occasionally. Serve kraut mixture with sliced roast pork.

Dis jus' got to be good. Dat's all dare is to it. If some of you friens' don' like dat I t'ink dey better call the doctor quick an' fast 'cause dey is plumb sick.

Special Oven-Fried Turkey

- 1 fryer-roaster turkey, 4 to 6 lbs. ready to cook weight, cut in serving pieces
- 1¼ cups melted butter (or margarine)
- salt and red pepper
- 2 cups seasoned bread crumbs
- ¼ tsp. bitters (Peychaud or Angostura)

Season turkey pieces with salt and red pepper. Dip in butter and bitters, then roll in crumbs. Place pieces, skin side up (not touching), in a greased baking pan. Drizzle with half of the remaining butter, and sprinkle with remaining crumbs. Cover the pan with aluminum foil.

Bake in a 350-degree oven for 1 hour. Uncover and pour remaining butter over turkey. Bake, uncovered, for 30 to 45 minutes longer, or until the meat is tender and brown. Makes six to eight servings.

Look, ma frien'. Don' argue wit' me about what we got cooked. Taste it an' see if it don' taste jus' like I tol' you it would.

Sweet-n-Sour Turkey Wings

6 turkey wings
2 cups water
1 rib celery
1 tsp. salt
¼ tsp. pepper
2 tbsp. plain flour
3 tbsp. olive oil
1½ cups chicken (or turkey) stock
½ cup vinegar
1/3 cup soy sauce
1/3 cup catsup (or chili sauce)
1 cup drained pineapple chunks
1 cup roll cut carrots
1 cup green pepper, cut into strips

Separate the turkey wings at the joints and discard tips. Wash, drain, and cook in water along with celery, salt, and pepper. Simmer, covered, over low heat until tender.

In the meantime, brown the flour and 1 tablespoon olive oil in a small saucepan. Add stock, vinegar, soy sauce, and catsup; cook and stir until thick. Set aside. Heat a large skillet and add 2 tablespoons olive oil. Fry carrots for 1 minute, stirring constantly. Add green pepper and pineapple and heat.

Blend together the sweet-n-sour sauce and tender wing pieces. Bring to a simmer. Serve hot over rice. Makes six servings.

Shoulder Beef Steak Etouffée

3 ½ to ¾ in. shoulder steaks
lemon pepper seasoning
3 slices chopped lime
2 cups chopped onion
1 cup chopped bell pepper
salt
soy sauce
red pepper
1 cup sauterne wine
parsley
garlic

Season meat with lemon pepper, salt, red pepper, and garlic. Put the meat in a pot, and add the rest of the ingredients. Cover and cook over a low fire. Get it real hot to start, then turn down and cook it slowly until the meat is done. And it is *delicious*!

Super-Sized Kraut-Stuffed Chops

2 tbsp. olive oil
6 thick loin pork chops with pockets
2 green peppers
1 cup chopped onion
6 cups drained sauerkraut
1 lb. carrots, peeled and shredded
1½ tsp. salt
¼ tsp. pepper
¼ tsp. dried mint
1 tbsp. sugar

Brown the chops on both sides in olive oil in a large ovenproof skillet. Remove chops and set aside.

Slice 4 rings from the green peppers and set aside; dice remaining green pepper. Sauté the diced pepper and onion in drippings until clear. Stir in carrots, and sauté 1 minute. Add seasonings, sugar, and sauerkraut; toss until combined.

Stuff each pork chop with some of the kraut mixture. Use small skewers (or sew with heavy thread) to close the opening. Place stuffed pork chops on top of the remaining kraut mixture in a baking pan. Cover and bake in a 325-degree oven for 45 minutes; uncover and bake 40 minutes longer or until chops are done.

Remove skewers or thread from chops before serving. Garnish with green pepper rings. Serves six.

Good Ol' Sausage

5 lbs. lean pork meat
2½ lbs. clear fat pork
½ tsp. sugar
¼ tsp. ginger
⅛ lb. fine salt
½ tsp. pepper
¼ tsp. dried mint

Cut meat into small pieces and season with sugar, ginger, salt, pepper, and mint. Put through a food chopper, using the sausage cutter, and grind twice.

Pack into sterilized jars and keep in a cool place. Use as wanted. This can be frozen, also, too.

Chicken

Baked Fryer

3½ to 4 lb. young fryer
flour
salt
pepper
2 onions, finely chopped
2 green peppers, chopped
1 small garlic bean, minced
1½ tsp. salt
½ tsp. red pepper
1 tsp. dried mint
2 No. 2 cans tomatoes
½ tsp. chopped parsley
½ tsp. powdered thyme
¼ lb. almonds, scalded, skinned, and roasted to golden brown
3 heaping tbsp. dried currants
2 cups cooked rice
cooking oil
parsley for garnish

Cut up the chicken in pieces for frying. Remove the skin and roll pieces in flour, salt, and pepper. Brown in oil. Take the chicken from the pan, but keep it hot. (This is a secret of the dish's success.)

Into the lard in which the chicken has been browned, put the onions, peppers, and garlic. Cook very slowly, stirring constantly. Season with salt, mint, and red pepper. Add tomatoes, parsley, and thyme.

Put the chicken in a roaster and pour the mixture over it. If the sauce does not cover the chicken, rinse out the skillet in which the mixture has been cooked and pour over chicken, also, too. Cover the roaster tightly. Bake in a moderate oven (325°) about 45 minutes, until the chicken is tender.

Place the chicken in the center of a large platter. Pile around it the rice, which has been cooked very dry. Drop currants into the sauce mixture and pour over the rice. Scatter almonds over the top. Garnish with parsley and you have food for the gods.

Me, I got a frien', an' his name is George Fairchild, who is the very firs' Jambalaya Festival King. An' he only use ash wood to cook dem jambalaya. I had to got me some from him an' rat quick 'cause I needed jambalaya cook for me an' some of ma good friens'. An' I wanna tol' you somet'ing. Mr. George can control dat fire aroun' dat wash pot better than I can gas on ma stove, I garontee!

Baked Chicken on a Sunday Cooked on a Tuesday a la Walter Guitreau

2 to 3 lbs. chicken
2 cups uncooked rice
1 can celery soup
1 can mushroom soup
1 envelope dried onion soup mix
2 soup cans milk

Skin and cut up the chicken into chunks. Pour the celery soup, mushroom soup, and milk over the rice and mix well. Empty the mixture into a 9-inch x 12-inch baking pan. Place the chicken on top, and sprinkle the onion soup over the whole mess. Cover with aluminum foil.

Bake in a 325-degree oven for 2 to 2½ hours. Just put it in there and forget about it. Bake until the chicken falls off the bone.

It was Walter's turn to cook for the bourree players while dey lose all our money. He called his dish Baked Chicken on a Sunday. But he made it on a Tuesday. It ain't not'ing in the world but baked jambalaya. An' it's delicious.

Yorkshire Chicken

1¼ cups flour
3 tsp. salt
1 tsp. ground sage
¼ tsp. red pepper
2½ to 3 lbs. chicken pieces, for frying
¼ cup oil
1 tsp. baking powder
3 eggs, well beaten
1½ cups milk
¼ cup melted butter (or margarine)
¼ cup chopped parsley

Combine ¼ cup flour, 2 teaspoons salt, the sage, and pepper in a bag. Add chicken, and shake, coating pieces evenly. Brown the chicken in oil on all sides in a large skillet. Remove to a deep 2-quart casserole.

Sift the remaining 1 cup flour, the baking powder, and remaining teaspoon of salt. Combine the eggs, milk, melted butter, and parsley. Blend with the flour mixture until smooth. Pour over chicken.

Bake at 350° for 1 hour or until done. Serves four.

Chicken Tetrazzini

3 tbsp. margarine
2 tbsp. plain flour
½ cup diced green pepper
½ lb. sliced fresh mushrooms
1 clove garlic, crushed
½ cup sauterne wine
1 envelope chunky chicken noodle soup mix
2 cups water
1 broiler-fryer chicken, cooked, boned, and cut into chunks
1¼ cups grated Parmesan cheese
¼ cup chopped parsley
8 oz. uncooked noodles

Melt margarine in a skillet. Add flour, and cook until it is brown and the flour taste is gone. Add green pepper; cook over low heat 4 minutes, stirring frequently. Stir in the mushrooms, and cook until tender. Remove from heat. Blend in the sauterne wine and garlic.

Bring water to a boil in a saucepan. Stir in the soup mix. Reduce heat; partially cover and simmer 5 minutes. Add chicken, 1 cup cheese, parsley, and vegetable mixtures, and heat.

Meanwhile, cook the noodles in boiling salted water according to the directions on the package. Drain. Arrange in the bottom of a greased 3-quart casserole. Cover with chicken sauce and stir lightly to mix. Sprinkle with remaining ¼ cup cheese. Broil until lightly browned on top, about 5 minutes. Makes seven servings.

Seafood

Crawfish Casserole

1 cup diced celery
½ cup crawfish fat (If you don't have it, use ¼ cup margarine.)
½ cup green onion tops
3 slices moistened bread
2 small cloves garlic
¼ cup margarine
1 cup water
bread crumbs
6 sprigs chopped parsley
2 cups cooked rice
1½ cups chopped onion
1 can (10½ oz.) mushroom soup
½ cup sauterne wine
⅓ cup chopped green pepper
2 cups crawfish tails
paprika

Sauté celery, onions, and bell pepper in crawfish fat (or margarine) until tender. Add green onion tops, soup, garlic, parsley, and crawfish tails. Heat slowly until hot. Add bread, rice, wine, and water and cook 15 minutes longer. Season to taste.

Turn the mixture into a 2-quart casserole dish. Dot with margarine; sprinkle with bread crumbs and paprika. Cover and bake in a 375-degree oven for 30 minutes. Serves eight.

Crawfish Etouffée

5 to 6 lbs. crawfish
1 lb. oleo
5½ lbs. chopped onion
4 cups bell pepper
4 cups parsley
2 tbsp. lemon juice
2 tbsp. Lea & Perrins
4 tsp. salt to taste (Don't add all at one time. Taste, then add.)
1 tbsp. Louisiana hot sauce (or ½ tsp. Tabasco)

Put oleo in pan. (Use crawfish fat if you have it.) Add chopped onions, bell pepper, parsley, Louisiana hot sauce, and Lea & Perrins. Season with salt and lemon juice. Simmer, covered, for an hour. (This will make its own juice.) Then add the crawfish and cook, covered, for 30 minutes to an hour.

I believe Walter jus' tol' Alma Picou dat the best sauce piquante he made was out of nutria rat, muskrat, an' coon all mixed together. But I don' exactly believe dat, no! I don' believe I don' believe dat too, also.

Barbecued Oysters

4 doz. oysters
½ cup chili powder
½ cup plain flour
1 tsp. cayenne pepper
1 tsp. garlic powder
1 tbsp. salt
1 tsp. hickory-smoked salt

Put the dry ingredients in a heavy paper bag and shake real well. Add oysters one at a time and shake. Fry in deep hot fat (about 360° to 365°) until done.

Crawfish Sauce Piquante

6 lbs. crawfish
26 oz. chopped onion
10 oz. chopped bell pepper
8 oz. celery
6 oz. green onion
7½ or 8 oz. parsley
1 tbsp. finely chopped garlic
2 cups flour
1 cup olive oil
½ cup Louisiana hot sauce
½ cup Lea & Perrins
3 tbsp. salt
2½ qts. water
2 cans (8 oz. each) tomato sauce
1 cup sauterne wine

Make a dark roux with the flour and olive oil. Add onion, pepper, and celery. Cook until the vegetables are clear. Add green onions and parsley and cook until juiced. Stir in the water, tomato sauce, garlic, hot sauce, Lea & Perrins, and salt.

If there is no fat on the crawfish, you should add ¼ pound oleo. Add the crawfish. Bring to a boil, and let simmer for about 2 hours.

Shrimp in Green Sauce over Rice

1½ lbs. raw shrimp, shelled and deveined
¼ cup butter (or margarine)
1/3 cup finely minced onion
3 tbsp. flour
2½ cups chicken broth
½ cup sauterne wine
½ cup minced parsley
pinch of cayenne pepper
½ cup sliced stuffed olives
6 cups hot, cooked rice
¼ tsp. bitters (Peychaud or Angostura)
2 tsp. soy sauce

Cook the shrimp in boiling, salted water until pink (about 4 minutes). Drain and set aside.

Melt the butter in a heavy saucepan; add onions and cook until soft, but not browned. Blend in flour. Gradually add chicken broth and wine; cook, stirring constantly, until the sauce thickens. Add parsley, cayenne pepper, olives, bitters, soy sauce, and shrimp. Simmer until thoroughly heated.

Serve over beds of hot rice. Makes six servings.

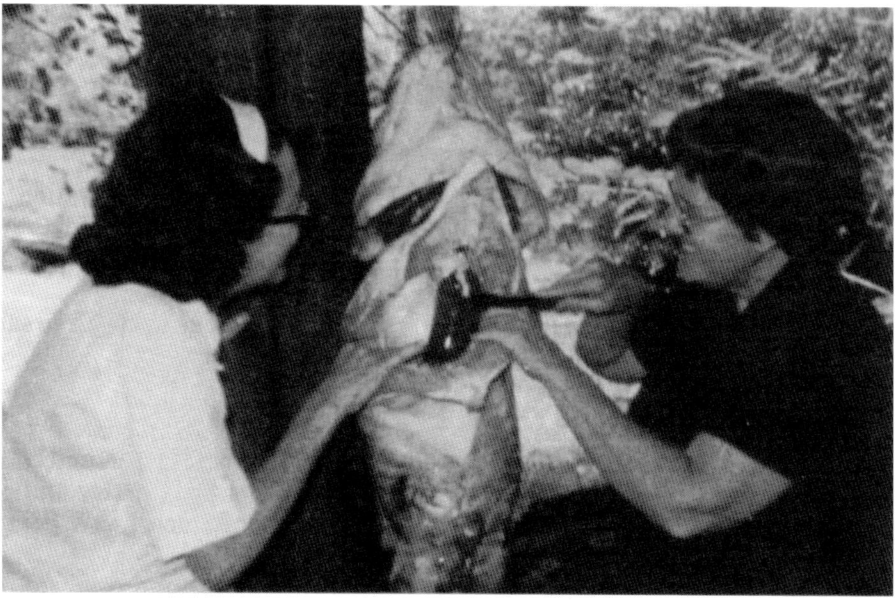

Ma wife Sara an' Walter's wife Maxine put dere selves here an' hep clean dat big spotted catfish.

Walter Guitreau caught dis forty fo' poun' catfish an' mos' fell overbode to got him in de bote. We made courtbouillon wit' de head, an serv' dat wit' rice, an' tol' ma grandson dat it was fish heads an' rice. An' dat's what it was, yeah!

Fish Courtbouillon a la Justin

3 cups chopped onion
2 cups chopped celery
1 cup chopped bell or sweet pepper
½ cup chopped parsley
2 cups chopped green onion (shallots)
1 tbsp. chopped garlic
5 or 6 cups fish, boned and skinned
2 tbsp. olive oil
2 cups grated carrots
¼ cup chopped lemon
2 cups sauterne wine
8 cups water
1 tbsp. soy sauce
1 tbsp. Worcestershire
2 tsp. Louisiana hot sauce (or 1 tsp. Tabasco)
¼ tsp. bitters (Peychaud or Angostura)
3 to 4 tsp. salt

Sauté or simmer the onions, celery, and bell pepper in olive oil until clear. Add parsley, green onion, garlic, and carrots and simmer for about 15 minutes. Pour in the lemon, wine, fish, and the remainder of the ingredients.

Bring to a boil, and let cook over low heat (nearly simmer) for 3 to 4 hours. Do not stir. This can be made with a light roux, also, too.

Shrimp a la Mexicana

1 lb. cooked shrimp
2 tsp. cooking oil
½ cup chopped celery
1 medium onion, chopped
1 can (6 oz.) whole, peeled tomatoes
3 cloves garlic, minced (or garlic powder to taste)
½ tsp. cayenne pepper
salt to taste
1 tsp. paprika
½ cup sauterne wine
1 tbsp. flour
1 cup grated cheddar cheese
½ cup chopped bell pepper

Sauté the onion, bell pepper, and celery in heated oil. Add the tomatoes, garlic, pepper, salt, paprika, wine, and flour. Blend well and simmer for 45 minutes. Add cooked shrimp and simmer for 15 minutes.

Serve over rice and top with grated cheese. Makes six to eight servings.

Mirliton Stuffed With Shrimp

STUFFING:
3 tbsp. margarine
2/3 cup finely chopped onion
2 cups medium shrimp, peeled and deveined
3 slices bread, soaked in water and squeezed
6 medium-sized mirliton
1/4 cup shallots
1/4 cup chopped parsley
1/4 tsp. red cayenne pepper
1 tsp. salt

TOPPING:
3 tbsp. melted margarine
1/4 cup plain bread crumbs

Cut mirliton in half lengthwise, and place in a pot of boiling water. Cover and boil for 15 minutes or until tender. Remove seeds and scoop out the pulp. Keep pulp and shells.

Sauté the onions in margarine for 5 minutes. Add mirliton pulp, bread, shallots, parsley, salt, and pepper. Continue cooking for approximately 10 minutes. Mix well, stirring constantly. Add shrimp.

Pile the mixture into mirliton shells. Top with buttered bread crumbs and bake 30 minutes at 350°. Serves six to eight.

Shrimp Mold

1 can condensed tomato soup
1 large pkg. cream cheese
2 pkg. unflavored gelatin
2 cups boiled shrimp, chopped
1 cup mayonnaise
4 or 5 green onions
salt
pepper
Tabasco sauce

Heat the soup to a boil. Stir in cream cheese. Dissolve gelatin in 1/2 cup water and add to the soup mix. Let cool. Add all other ingredients (except shrimp).

Place in the mold in layers of sauce and shrimp. Chill until mold is set.

Garfish Balls

2 cups flour
1 cup oil
2 onions, chopped fine
1 potato
1 can tomato sauce
½ cup tomato catsup
4 eggs, beaten
1 bell pepper, chopped
6 cups ground garfish
1 red pepper
salt and pepper to taste
onion tops
parsley

Grind one onion for the roux and set aside.

Grind the fish, one onion, potato, and red pepper. (Scrape the fish from the skin and bone before grinding, using a spoon of some kind.) Mix well, and add the eggs and salt and pepper to taste.

Form into balls. (Wet your hands occasionally so the fish won't stick to your hands.) Fry the balls until brown.

Make a roux with the flour and olive oil. Add water, tomato sauce, tomato catsup, and bell pepper. Let simmer for 1 hour. Add fishballs, onion tops, and parsley, and cook another hour. Serve hot.

I'll never forgot dat firs' batch we made, no. Ooh boy! Dey was so hard, nobody would eat 'em! Not even the dogs would touch 'em! But dey did make good golf balls, I garontee!

Baked and Broiled Oysters

large oysters
Pam
seasoned salt
lemon pepper seasoning
Worcestershire sauce

Drain the oysters well and place one layer in a baking pan. (Spray the pan with Pam first.) Sprinkle with seasoned salt and lemon pepper seasoning. Dash Worcestershire sauce on each oyster. Bake at 250° for 15 to 20 minutes, then broil until brown.

Dose catfish what Murphy Brown hold up dare for me, dey jus' the good eatin' size. You can filet dem if you want an' you can steak dem if you want. An' I axed Murphy where he got dose. An' he tol' me, an' I believe him also, too.

Fried Catfish

10 lbs. catfish
cooking oil
2½ cups cornmeal
ground red cayenne pepper
1 tsp. butter-flavored salt
1 cup milk
1 cup plain flour
salt
1 tsp. garlic powder

Soak catfish in milk. Mix the dry ingredients thoroughly in a bowl or bag. Roll the fish in dry ingredients. Fry in hot cooking oil deep enough to float the fish. (Be sure grease or oil is not too hot.)

Catfish Manchac a la Walter and Justin

self-rising flour
seasoned cornmeal
salt
red pepper
2 eggs
1 qt. milk
catfish
Louisiana hot sauce

Slice the catfish thin when it is half-thawed. Marinate for 2 to 3 hours in Louisiana hot sauce. Drain.

Mix together equal parts of flour and seasoned cornmeal. Season that cornmeal with salt, red pepper, garlic powder, chili powder, onion powder, lemon pepper seasoning, and anything else you want to throw in there. Mix together the eggs and milk.

Dip the fish in the milk mixture, then in the dry mix. (Be sure the fish is completely thawed before dipping.) Deep fry at about 365° until fish floats to the top. Bread only as needed, right before frying.

Shrimp Stew

3 lbs. shrimp, peeled and deveined
4 medium onions, chopped
½ cup chopped bell pepper
½ cup chopped celery
1 clove garlic, finely chopped
1 cup chopped parsley (or ½ cup dried parsley)
1 cup flour
½ cup olive oil
salt
red pepper

Use an iron pot, if possible. Heat the cooking oil, add flour, and cook to a dark brown over a low fire. Be sure to keep stirring this mixture constantly. If the phone rings, don't answer.

Add chopped seasoning, and simmer over low heat about 1 hour.

Season the shrimp with salt and red pepper and add to the sauce mixture. Cover and simmer together for about ½ hour. (Keep the heat low.) Add 3 cups water, cover, and continue to simmer over low heat for about 1 more hour.

Serve over rice. Serves six to eight.

Broiled Oysters

large oysters
Pam
salt
lemon pepper seasoning
butter-flavored salt
sauterne wine

Spray a baking pan with Pam. Sprinkle salt, butter-flavored salt, and lemon pepper over each oyster. Put a little wine on the bottom of the pan to use for basting. Add oysters and broil until done. Eat as soon as they come out of the oven.

Broiled Red Snapper

3 sticks butter (or margarine)
juice of 2 lemons
1 tbsp. Worcestershire
2 tbsp. olive oil
1 tsp. salt
½ tsp. Louisiana hot sauce
red snapper

Place the red snapper in a greased pan. Broil for 15 to 25 minutes.

Heat the butter, lemon juice, Worcestershire, olive oil, salt, and hot sauce in a pan. Never bring to a boil. Pour over the fish when served.

Barbecued Crabs

6 crab bodies
½ cup chili powder
½ cup plain flour
1 tsp. ground cayenne pepper
1 tsp. garlic powder
1 tbsp. salt
1 tsp. hickory-smoked salt
cooking oil

Put the dry ingredients in a heavy paper bag and shake to mix. Add crab bodies one at a time and shake. Fry crabs in deep, hot fat (about 360° to 365°) until done.

Game

Wild Ducks and Turnips

- 4 to 6 wild ducks
- 1 cup celery
- 1 tbsp. minced garlic
- 3 cups chopped onion
- 1 cup sweet pepper
- 1 cup chopped green onion
- 1 cup flour
- 1 cup cooking oil
- 4 to 6 cups water
- 1 cup parsley
- 1 tbsp. Lea & Perrins
- 1 tbsp. soy sauce
- ½ tbsp. bitters (Peychaud or Angostura)
- 2 tsp. hot sauce
- salt to taste
- 3 cups sauterne wine
- 6 to 8 cups chopped turnips

Brown off the ducks and put in a pot big enough to cook the whole meal.

Make a roux with the flour and oil. After the roux is made, stir in chopped onions, celery, and sweet pepper and cook until the vegetables are clear. Then add 4 to 6 cups of water, the wine, and the other seasonings. Pour this over the ducks and turnips. Cook 4 to 6 hours over a low fire.

I need to tol' you somet'ing here. Don' you try an' use live decoys to caught dem duck. You would have a helluva time tryin' to teach live decoys to play dead! But when you caught dem duck, you can make you some fine duck an' turnip. An' I wanna tol' you somet'ing else, too, also. I know people who will quit there jobs to eat dis. Like dis fella from Lafayette. I tol' him I'm fixin' to cook duck an' turnip. He say, "Forget about what I'm doin' here, I'm on my way rat now." An' he come on down rat here to eat dose duck.

You see dat duck on dat island dare? Dat would make real good duck an' turnip. Oooh boy! But you know somet'ing? Sara would kill *me* if I killed dat duck!

Pork and Deer Sausage

- 1¾ lbs. ground deer meat
- 1¾ lbs. ground pork (Be sure it's fat.)
- 1 tbsp. salt
- 1 tsp. red cayenne pepper
- ⅛ tsp. garlic powder
- 1 tsp. cumin
- 1 tsp. poultry seasoning
- ⅛ tsp. sage
- ⅛ tsp. curry powder
- 1 tsp. dried mint

Mix all of the ingredients well and make into patties. Be sure you don't mix more than 3½ pounds at a time with this particular recipe.

NOTE: It's a good idea to grind the pork and venison together. Grind twice.

Squirrel Stew

- 3 or 4 squirrels
- 2 cups chopped onions
- 1 cup chopped green onion
- 1 cup chopped bell pepper
- 1½ cups chopped celery
- 2 cloves garlic, chopped
- ½ cup parsley (or ¼ cup dried parsley)
- 1 tbsp. soy sauce
- 2 tsp. salt and pepper (to taste)
- 1 cup sauterne wine
- 1 dash bitters (Peychaud or Angostura)
- 2 cups water
- 1 tsp. Louisiana hot sauce

Some people like to brown the squirrel off before they cook it. Either way, first you make a roux, with ½ cup bacon drippings and ¾ cup flour. Get it as dark as you like it, which should be pretty dark.

Cook the onions, celery, and bell peppers until clear. Add green onions and parsley. Pour in the water, wine, hot sauce, bitters, garlic, and soy sauce. Put the squirrel in last and cook the whole darn mess a few hours or so over a low fire.

Les' see dare now. I can't make up ma head whether we're gonna serv' dis rabbit sauce piquante wit' spaghetti or wit' rice. Dey are both some wondermous, I garontee!

Rabbit Sauce Piquante

4 lbs. rabbit, cut in 2-in. cubes
8 medium onions, chopped
2 bunches green onions, chopped
1 large bell pepper, chopped
1 cup chopped celery
2 cans (8 oz. each) tomato sauce
1 cup olive oil
2 cloves garlic, chopped
2 tbsp. Worcestershire
juice of 2 lemons
¾ cup bacon drippings
1 cup all-purpose flour (for roux)
salt
6 cups water
black pepper
red cayenne pepper
¼ tsp. bitters
2 cups sauterne wine

Wash the rabbit, season with salt and pepper, and fry in bacon drippings until brown. Remove from fat and set aside. Make a roux, using the olive oil, flour, and tomato sauce. (See my recipe in the front of the book.)

Add all the chopped seasoning except garlic, cover, and simmer on low heat for about 1 hour. Add the rabbit to the roux and chopped seasoning mixture and simmer for 30 minutes, covered.

Stir in water, bitters, wine, lemon juice, and garlic, cover, and let cook slowly for about 2 more hours.

Serve over rice or spaghetti.

Rabbit Etouffée

1 cup olive oil
1 domestic or wild rabbit, cut up
3 cups chopped onion
1 cup chopped celery
1 cup chopped bell pepper
½ cup chopped parsley
2 tbsp. Worcestershire
1 tsp. Louisiana hot sauce
salt
ground red cayenne pepper
2 cups sauterne wine
1 tbsp. chopped garlic

In a Dutch oven, brown off the rabbit in olive oil. Add all of the other ingredients. Salt and pepper to taste. Cover and let cook over low heat for 2 hours.

I'm trimmin the fat from dem venison roast dare 'cause fat on venison don' taste good, no. An' you can look at Sara an' see she's kinda nervous about the way I'm do dis. But we'll get it did, jus' the same.

Cooking in a Bag

There are several things you should remember when cooking in a bag. Follow these safety factors an' you will have no problems, I garontee.

1. Check the bag to see if there are any holes in the bottom (of the bag, that's right). If so, don't use.
2. Always put 1 tablespoon flour (at least) in the bag and shake it up real good before you add anything else.
3. Punch holes in the top of the bag with a 2-tine kitchen fork. Punch about 12 holes each time.
4. Never cook in an oven over 350°.

Also, too, cooking in a bag is a great energy saver. Your meat cooks in about 1/3 less time than usual and stays more moist in the bag.

Backbone Pork and Mushrooms

8 backbones (each cut 1 in. thick)
1 lb. fresh mushrooms
2 tsp. garlic powder
red cayenne pepper
salt
2 cups chopped onion
2 tbsp. all-purpose flour
2 tbsp. dry parsley flakes
1 tbsp. Lea & Perrins
¼ tsp. bitters (Peychaud or Angostura)
2 cups sauterne wine
1 14-in. x 20-in. clear baking bag

Season the meat with salt and pepper. Put the flour in the baking bag and shake. Place the meat in the bag, with a sprinkle of parsley and garlic powder. Add the onions and mushrooms. Stir Lea & Perrins and bitters into the wine, and pour over the meat.

Close and tie the bag and punch 12 holes in it with a 2-tine kitchen fork. Cook in a 325-degree oven until brown.

Beef Shanks in a Bag

2 tbsp. flour
salt
ground red cayenne pepper
6 shank bones, cut 2½ to 3 in. thick
12 whole medium carrots
2 pounds potatoes, cut in half
6 small onions, cut in half
4 whole cloves garlic
1 can Ro Tel
1 tbsp. soy sauce
2 tbsp. Worcestershire
½ tsp. bitters (Peychaud or Angostura)
2 cups sauterne wine
turkey size cooking bag

Beef shanks are the cheapest cut of meat you can buy, and also the most tasty, because they are next to the bone.

Grease pan. Put 2 tablespoons flour in a turkey bag and shake, coating sides well. Place the bag in the pan. Salt and red pepper the shanks. Put shanks in the bag, and place the vegetables over and around them evenly.

Combine Ro Tel sauce, soy sauce, Worcestershire, bitters, and sauterne wine. Mix well and pour over the shanks and vegetables. Tie the bag and punch 12 holes in the top with a cooking fork. Cook at 325° for 2 hours.

Pork Roast

pork roast (at least 5 lb.)
peppers
shallots
garlic
salt
ground red cayenne pepper
2 tbsp. flour
1 cup chopped green onion
1 cup wine
2 cups water

Cut holes in various places on the roast and stuff with peppers, shallots, and garlic on both sides. Salt and red pepper both sides of the roast.

Grease pan. Shake flour in the cooking bag, coating sides well. Place in the bag the stuffed roast, chopped green onion, wine, and the water. Close and tie the bag, and punch 9 times with a 2-tine kitchen fork. Put the whole mess in the pan, and bake at 325° for 3 hours.

Pot Roast Magnifique

8 lb. chuck roast
6 whole cloves garlic
6 pickled hot peppers
6 shallots
salt
red pepper
8 whole potatoes
8 whole carrots
4 whole onions
1 lb. fresh mushrooms
2 tbsp. Worcestershire
2 cups wine
2 tbsp. flour
¼ tsp. bitters (Peychaud or Angostura)

Grease pan. Put 2 tablespoons flour in a cooking bag and shake, coating sides evenly.

Salt and pepper the roast. Cut holes in the roast, and stuff each with garlic, a green pepper, and a shallot. (Cut off the portion of the pepper and shallot sticking out of the hole.)

Place stuffed chuck roast in a large cooking bag and then put it in the pan. Add to the bag, placing around the roast evenly potatoes, carrots, onions, and mushrooms. Mix the Worcestershire sauce, bitters, and wine. Pour over the ingredients in the bag and tie.

Punch 12 holes in the top of the bag with a 2-tine fork. Bake at 350° for about 2 or 3 hours.

Ooh boy! Magnifique mean magnificent. An' dat's exactly how it taste, marvelmous, I garontee!

Turkey in a Bag

Clean the turkey well, both inside and out. Sprinkle with salt and pepper. Grease your turkey. Put 1 tablespoon flour in a large cooking bag and shake it up. Put the turkey in the bag, tie, and punch 9 holes with a kitchen fork. Cook at 325° until the turkey browns.

You can put potatoes around the turkey if you want. (Actually, you can put anything next to it and it will taste good!) Also, too, you can put dressing in the turkey. But don' you forget to sew it up.

Sittin' rat in front of dat beautiful roast what I got dare are two of the reasons why twin beds were invent. Dem are onions. An' what I'm sayin' here is you took ma onion away from me, an' I can't cook not'ing hardly none at all any.

Boned Rump Roast in a Bag

- 1 tbsp. flour
- 10-lb. roast beef, tied
- 4 lbs. mushrooms
- 5 cloves garlic
- 5 green onions (shallots)
- 5 hot pickled peppers
- 1 cup chopped green onion
- ½ cup chopped parsley
- 2 tbsp. soy sauce
- 8 medium Irish potatoes
- ½ tsp. bitters (Peychaud or Angostura)
- ground red cayenne pepper
- salt
- 8 large carrots
- 1 tsp. celery seed
- 2 tbsp. olive oil
- 2 cups sauterne wine
- 1 cup water

Stuff garlic, onions, and peppers in five holes deep into the roast. Clean the mushrooms well. Salt and pepper the roast. Place the roast in a cooking bag with 1 tablespoon flour shaken up in it. Put the mushrooms, carrots, and potatoes around the roast. (Sprinkle a little salt on them first.) Add parsley, green onion, celery seed, and olive oil. Pour in the wine, water, soy sauce, and bitters.

Tie the bag and punch 9 times with a 2-tine kitchen fork. Cook for 1½ hours at 350°.

Quail in a Bag

- 1 tbsp. flour
- 6 quail
- salt
- ground red cayenne pepper
- 1 cup chopped onion
- ½ cup chopped bell pepper
- 1 lb. fresh mushrooms
- bay leaf
- 1 cup sauterne wine
- ½ lemon
- 1 cup water

Grease pan. Put 1 tablespoon flour in a large cooking bag and shake well, coating sides evenly.

Split dressed birds down the back. Salt and red pepper them, rubbing seasonings well into the birds. Put the birds in the bag. Add all the other ingredients to the bag and tie.

Punch 12 holes in the top of the bag with a 2-tine fork. Bake at 350° for 45 minutes. Serves four to six.

Dat's Mac DeArmand tellin' me how he cook a goose. An' you can tol' I don' believe one damn word what he sayin', 'cause I believe his goose is cooked!

Beef Ribs in a Bag

4 to 6 ribs (each 4 in. long)
seasoned salt
red cayenne pepper
1 tsp. garlic powder
2 tsp. onion powder
1 cup water
2 tbsp. Lea & Perrins
1 cup sauterne wine
salt
1 tbsp. flour

Salt and pepper the ribs with cayenne pepper, salt, and seasoned salt. Place in a large plastic baking bag with flour shaken up in it. Mix wine, water, Lea & Perrins, garlic powder, and onion powder in a mixing bowl until the powders are dissolved. Pour into the bag around the ribs.

Tie the bag and punch 12 times with a 2-tine kitchen fork. Cook in 325-degree oven for 1 hour.

Wild Goose in a Bag

1 or 2 large geese
6 large onions
10 small potatoes
1 pkg. large, fresh mushrooms
2 cloves garlic
3 cups sauterne wine
2 tbsp. Lea & Perrins
1 tbsp. soy sauce
1 tsp. celery salt
1 cup water
salt and red pepper to taste
¼ tsp. bitters (Peychaud or Angostura)
turkey size cooking bag
1 tbsp. flour

Shake 1 tablespoon flour in the cooking bag, coating all sides well. Put the goose in the bag, and surround it with onions, mushrooms, and potatoes. Mix together the sauterne wine, Lea & Perrins, soy sauce, garlic, celery salt, water, and bitters. Pour the sauce over the goose.

Put everything in the bag and tie. Punch 12 holes in the bag with a 2-tine kitchen fork. Cook at 325° to 350° until you look in there and see that it's done. Cook some rice on the side to serve with it.

I got to tol' you somet'ing. I was trainin' a man to be a safety engineer down in South Louisiana. He look at me one day and say, "Justin, you know what a wild goose is?" I say, "What." He say, "About dat far off center!" I started to kill 'em.

Meat Loaf

3 lbs. ground round
1 tbsp. ground celery seed
1 tsp. garlic powder
1 tsp. dried mint
1 tbsp. Lea & Perrins
1 tsp. seasoned salt
1 tsp. salt
1 tbsp. parsley flakes
2 cups chopped onion
1 cup chopped green onion
1 cup chopped bell pepper
4 eggs, beaten well
¼ tsp. bitters (Peychaud or Angostura)
1 tsp. Louisiana hot sauce (or ½ tsp. Tabasco)

Get you the biggest bowl you can find in your house and mix all your ingredients together, except the eggs, Lea & Perrins, Louisiana hot sauce, and bitters. In a separate bowl mix the Lea & Perrins, hot sauce, and bitters with the eggs and beat real well. Mix all in the meat loaf.

Some people like a red sauce over meat loaf and some like brown. For the red sauce, mix 2 cans (16 oz. each) tomato sauce, and for the brown, mix 4 cans (8 oz. each) mushroom sauce. Pour either desired over the meat loaf. If necessary, add a little water and a little sauterne wine (in equal amounts).

Put 1 tablespoon flour in a cooking bag and shake it up real good. Put the whole damn thing in the bag and tie. The meat loaf will cook in about a third less time in the bag than usual. (Don't forget to punch holes in the cooking bag with a 2-tine kitchen fork!)

Cook for about 1 hour (or until it's brown) in a 325-degree oven.

Le' me tol' you somet'ing about dat meat loaf. It's one of dem Cajun dish what taste even better the nex' day on sammiches. It soak up all dem seasoning, an' it's good. (Dat depend if dey any lef', which I doubt.)

Chicken I Don't Know

turkey size cooking bag
2 tbsp. flour
2 big fryers, quartered
salt
ground red cayenne pepper
4 cups chopped onion
1 cup chopped celery
1 cup chopped bell pepper
1 cup water
1 cup chopped parsley
1 tbsp. chopped garlic
1 small bay leaf
1½ cups sauterne wine
1 tbsp. soy sauce
1 tbsp. Worcestershire
½ tsp. bitters (Peychaud or Angostura)

Grease pan. Put 2 tablespoons of flour in the bag and shake, coating sides well. Put the bag in the pan. Salt and pepper the fryers and place in bag. Add the onion, celery, bell pepper, parsley, garlic, and bay leaf.

Combine the sauterne, soy sauce, Worcestershire sauce, and bitters. Pour over the ingredients in the cooking bag. Pour 1 cup water over the ingredients in the cooking bag and tie.

Punch 12 holes in the top of the bag with a cooking fork. Bake at 350° for 1½ hours or until the chicken comes off the bone.

By the way, quartered means each fryer cut in 4 piece!

Chicken I Don't Know. I mus' tol' you about dis. I didn't know what the hell to call it! But I know one t'ing about it. It sure taste good, I garontee!

Egg Dishes

Baked Eggs

eggs
muffin tin
olive oil
Benedictine, Cointreau, creme de menthe, or brandy

Put a drop or two of olive oil and one egg in each muffin tin. In each egg, put a couple of drops of either Benedictine, Cointreau, creme de menthe, or brandy.

Bake at about 325°. Watch them and take them out when they are as hard as you like them.

I like eggs mos' anyway, 'cept raw. Dese are "good eggs," I garontee!

Peppy Pickled Eggs

18 to 20 large eggs
1 bay leaf
6 to 8 hot peppers
4 cloves garlic, cut in half
2 tbsp. salt
1 tbsp. chili powder
apple cider vinegar
water

After boiling the eggs, puncture several times with a toothpick. Put the eggs into jars. Place bay leaf, pepper, and garlic with the eggs. Repeat the layers until all of the ingredients are used. Add salt and chili powder.

Fill each jar with heated vinegar and water (half and half). (Don't boil the vinegar and water.) Cover the jar up completely. Seal the jar, invert, and shake well to mix the seasonings.

Wait a week before eating. These will keep at least 3 weeks in the refrigerator.

Rice Omelet (Egg Jambalaya)

bacon drippings
3 eggs, beaten well
½ cup chopped green onion
½ cup cooked rice

Put bacon drippings in an omelet pan. Pour in the beaten eggs, rice, and onion. Cook until the eggs are done.

Anchovy Omelet

4 eggs
1 clove garlic
1 tsp. chopped parsley
¾ tsp. anchovy paste

Beat the eggs. Rub a small bowl with garlic. Put the eggs in the bowl and stir in the parsley and anchovy paste. Cook in a greased omelet pan over medium fire until firm.

Omelet and Sausages

4 eggs
6 breakfast sausages

Broil 6 breakfast sausages, and drain them on absorbent paper. Keep them hot. Beat the eggs, and cook in an omelet pan over medium heat. Place the sausages on the omelet and fold it over. Garnish with parsley and serve with tomato sauce.

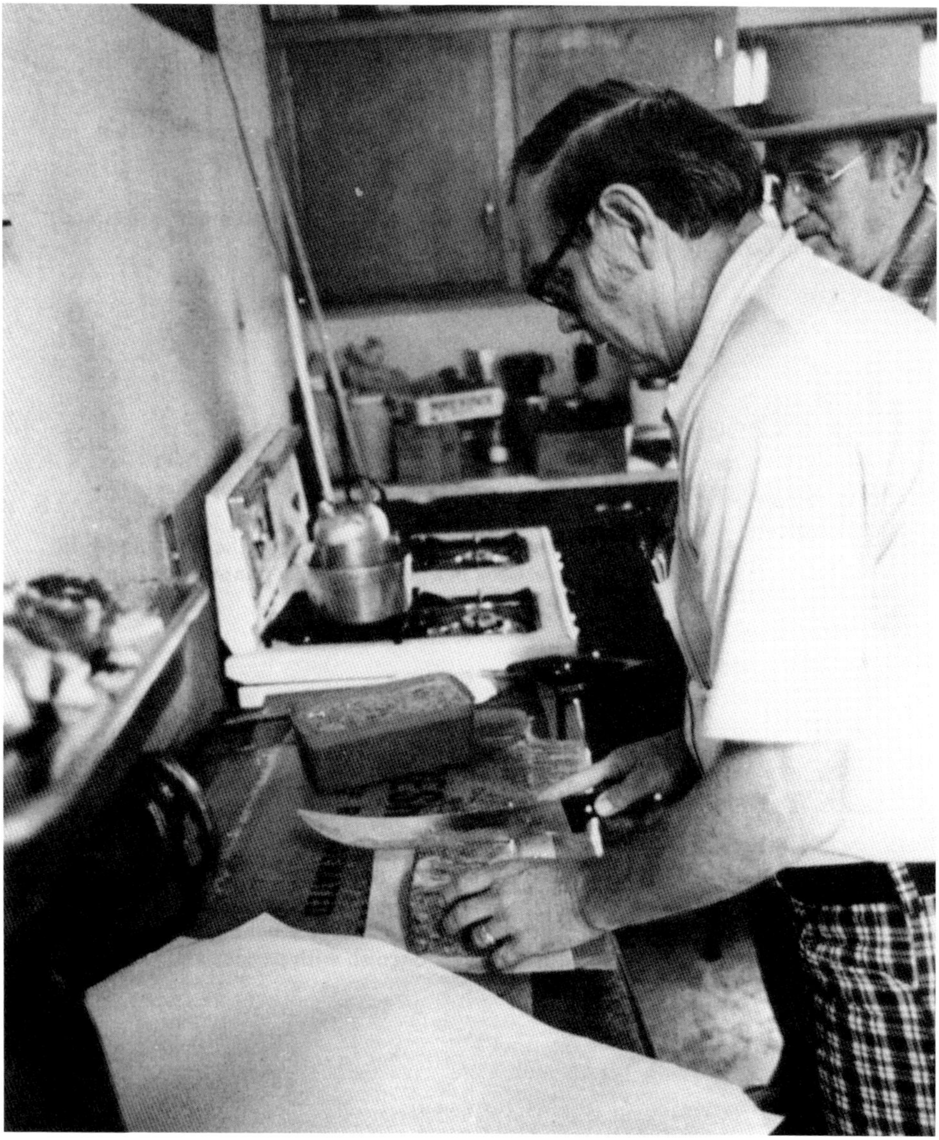

Murphy Brown, he put the insist on me dat I should try some of dis hogshead cheese what he's slicin' up. An' dat was a mistake wit' him. I done ate the whole damn t'ing!

Cheese Omelet

4 eggs
½ cup grated cheese
2 tbsp. chopped parsley
2 tbsp. chopped green pepper (if desired)

Beat the eggs. Sprinkle with cheese, parsley, and green pepper, and pour into a small casserole dish.

Bake the omelet in a slow oven (275°) until the cheese is melted. Serve with a parsley garnish.

Omelet with Creole Sauce and Peas

4 eggs
2 cups condensed tomato soup
2 tbsp. butter
½ cup chopped green pepper
2 cups cooked peas
½ cup chopped onion
½ cup chopped celery
½ cup chopped olives
½ cup chopped pickles

Beat 4 eggs. Cook the eggs in an omelet pan over medium heat. Mix together the rest of the ingredients. Pour the sauce around the omelet when cooked. Serve with a parsley garnish.

Lobster or Crabmeat Omelet

4 eggs
1 tbsp. minced onion
2 tbsp. butter (or bacon drippings)
1 tbsp. chopped celery (or more, if desired)
¾ cup diced lobster (or crabmeat)

Beat the eggs and cook in an omelet pan over medium heat. Sauté the onion in the butter. Add celery and lobster (or crabmeat) and simmer for 3 minutes. Before folding the omelet, spread it with the mixture. Fold and serve garnished with parsley.

Firm Omelet

4 eggs
4 tbsp. water
½ tsp. salt
⅛ tsp. paprika
1½ tbsp. butter

Beat the eggs until well blended. Add water, salt, and paprika. Melt 1½ tablespoons of butter in a skillet. When this is fairly hot, add the egg mixture and cook over low heat. (It is best to cook it in an omelet pan over a medium fire.)

Lift the edges of the omelet with a pancake turner and tilt the skillet to permit the uncooked custard to run to the bottom. When it is all an even consistency, increase the heat to brown the bottom slightly. Fold over the omelet and serve.

If you don' got no omelet pan, dat's bad. It take practice to fold over dem egg an' make dat omelet purty an' nice. You put dem egg dare in a plain ol' pan an' it's gonna run all over hell an' back.

Quiche Lorraine

4 eggs, slightly beaten
2 cups grated cheddar or Swiss cheese
½ cup chopped onions
2 tbsp. chopped pimento
2 tbsp. chopped bell peppers
2 unbaked pie shells
8 strips bacon, crumbled
paprika
1½ cups half-and-half (milk/cream)
1 cup chopped ham
salt
pepper
2 tbsp. flour

Blend all of the ingredients together and pour into unbaked pie shells. Bake at 400° for 15 to 20 minutes, or until firm and stiff.

Vegetables

Rice (Long Grain)

Place as much rice as you need in a heavy pan. Cover with enough water to measure first finger joint deep above the level of the rice. Use the middle finger to measure, since the first joint of the middle finger is the same length in every normal-sized adult, believe it or not! Add salt to taste, usually about 2 teaspoonfuls. Place over the hottest flame you can get and let it come to a rapid boil. Boil the rice until you can't see any water bubbling in the holes which will appear in the surface.

Then simmer for 30 to 40 minutes, with the pan lid on. Don't even peek at the rice until you're ready to serve it. Above all, don't panic. If you follow this recipe carefully, you won't burn a damn t'ing, I garontee!

Barbecued Beans

4 cans (16 oz. each) pork and beans
¾ lb. ground beef
½ lb. hot sausage (patty)
1 tsp. cayenne pepper
¾ cup molasses or honey
¾ cup barbecue sauce
8 to 10 slices crisp bacon
1 tbsp. Lea & Perrins
½ tsp. salt
couple good dashes of Louisiana hot sauce
1½ cups finely chopped onion
½ tsp. bitters (Peychaud or Angostura)
1 tsp. dried mint
1 tsp. liquid smoke

Cook ground beef and sausage until well done. Make it into a fine texture with a fork while cooking. Drain off the fat. Cook bacon crisp and crush over the other meats just cooked.

Open bean cans and drain off what juice you can. Mix the meats and all other ingredients with the beans. Bake in a pyrex or other oven bowl at 350° for 45 minutes. Serve hot.

Each time this stuff is reheated, it seems to taste better. It also freezes very well for later use. This stuff is plenty good, I garontee!

Black-Eyed Peas

1 lb. black-eyed peas
2 large onions, chopped
2 cloves garlic, chopped
1 green hot pepper, chopped (or 1½ tsp. Louisiana hot sauce) (or 1 tsp. Tabasco)
salt
sauterne wine
water
½ cup olive oil
¼ pound ham, salt shoulder, or pickled shoulder of pork

Wash peas well, getting all the grit and rocks out of them. Place in an earthenware or glass bowl. Add chopped onion, garlic, and pepper to the peas. Pour a mixture of ½ wine and ½ water over the peas so they are covered by an inch or more of liquid. Let soak overnight. You may have to add 1 cup wine and 1 cup water to them before you go to bed or before you put them on in the morning.

The next morning, cover the bottom of a heavy pot (preferably iron) with about ½ cup olive oil. Add the meat you have decided to use and heat. Pour peas and the mixture in which they have marinated into the pot. (Add water if necessary.) Bring to a good boil, then turn the fire down and cook slowly for several hours until done. Add salt just before the peas are done. Cook a few minutes longer, so the salt will be absorbed.

Serve over steamed rice. Serves four to six or maybe eight.

Broccoli With Rice

½ cup bacon drippings
1 onion, chopped fine
1 celery leaf, chopped fine
Tabasco sauce
salt
red pepper
1 pkg. chopped broccoli
1½ cups cooked rice
1 can cream of chicken soup
1 large cheese whiz
seasoned bread crumbs

Sauté the onion and celery in bacon drippings. Boil the broccoli and drain; mix with soup and cheese. Add the onion and celery. Stir in the rice, and season with salt and pepper to taste. Sprinkle seasoned bread crumbs on top.

Bake in a greased casserole at 325° for 45 minutes.

Stuffed Cucumbers

8 cucumbers, sliced lengthwise
2 tbsp. olive oil
½ cup chopped celery
1 heaping tbsp. dried parsley
½ cup chopped fresh mushroom stems (parboil until tender)
1½ cups chopped onion
1 large clove garlic, minced
1 cup chopped canned shrimp
1 cup seasoned bread crumbs
1 tbsp. Worcestershire
2 tsp. salt
2 tsp. Louisiana hot sauce (or 1 tsp. Tabasco)
½ cup sauterne wine
Romano cheese

Cut the cucumbers in half, and parboil in water until tender. Scrape the insides out and chop up in a bowl. Sauté in olive oil the onion, celery, parsley, and garlic after it has a little juice. Pour ½ cup wine and ½ cup water in a baking dish.

Stir all of the ingredients together. Stuff each cucumber shell with the mixture, and sprinkle with Romano cheese. Bake at 350° until brown (less than 1 hour).

Dis stuffed cucumbers, people laugh at me about dis. Dis dish was what come out of the kitchen after I got t'rough foolin' around dare for awhile. The secret is to use what you got. You could use anyt'ing an' it will turn out good. I believe you could t'row in a old shoe an' it won't be bad, no! I garontee it will be the mos' bes' t'ing you ate ever.

Green Tomato Casserole a la Justin

olive oil
6 green tomatoes, sliced thick
onions, sliced thin
salt
Season-all
Romano cheese, grated
bacon, sliced thick
seasoned bread crumbs

Place a small amount of olive oil in a casserole with thick-sliced tomatoes, thin-sliced onions, salt, and Season-all. Add Romano cheese. Add another layer above, and season with Season-all. Top with bread crumbs and sliced bacon. Cook 1 hour at 325°.

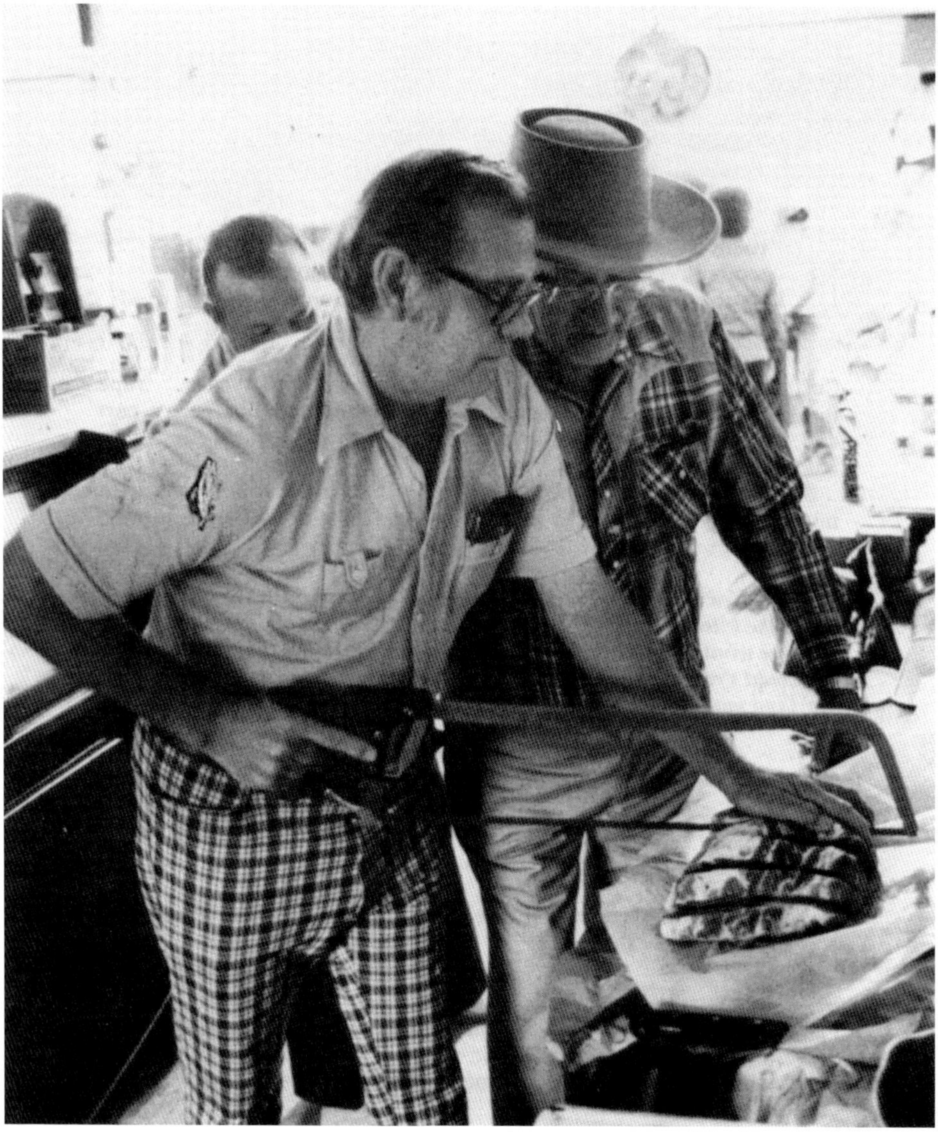

You noted dat I'm overlook real good dare to see dat Murphy Brown cut dis pickled shoulder of pig jus' rat for me so's I can season some good mustard greens an' cabbage an' all kinds vegetables like dat.

Red Beans With Rice and Smoked Sausage

1 lb. red kidney beans
2 large onions
2 cloves garlic
1 green hot pepper (or ½ tsp. Louisiana hot sauce)
claret wine
water
olive oil
¼ lb. ham, salt shoulder, or pickled shoulder of pork
salt
2 lbs. smoked sausage

Wash beans well, getting all grit and rocks out. Place in earthenware or glass bowl. Chop up onions, garlic, and pepper and add to the beans. If you no got pepper, add Louisiana hot sauce. Pour mixture of one half wine and one half water over beans so they are well covered by an inch or more of liquid. Let the beans soak or marinate overnight. You may have to add 1 cup wine and 1 cup water to them by bedtime or before you cook them in the morning.

The next morning, cover the bottom of a heavy pot with about ½ cup olive oil. Add sausage and the meat you decide to use and heat. Pour the beans and marinade mixture into the pot, along with some water, if necessary. Bring to a good boil, turn fire down, and cook slowly several hours until done. Add salt just before beans are done, and let cook. Serve over steamed rice. Serves four to six.

This recipe may also be applied to white or pinto beans, or dried peas, using sauterne in place of claret.

Squash Delight

1 lb. sliced yellow squash
½ cup green pepper
½ cup celery
½ cup onion (½ green, if available)
1 can water chestnuts, sliced
½ cup mayonnaise
½ cup oleo (if desired)
salt
red pepper
½ cup cheese
bread crumbs

Boil sliced squash just until tender. Drain. Add the rest of the ingredients. Pour into a casserole dish and top with bread crumbs. Bake for 45 minutes at 325°.

Red Beans and Rice au Vin

2 lbs. red beans, washed thoroughly and drained
½ cup olive oil
2 slices thick bacon, cubed
2 medium onions, chopped
1 small clove garlic, chopped
2 to 3 cups sauterne wine
1 tbsp. Worcestershire
1 to 2 tsp. Louisiana hot sauce
salt
water (if needed)

Marinate beans in water, wine, and seasonings (except salt) mixture overnight.

The next day, pour olive oil into a pot big enough to hold all of the beans with ease. Fry the bacon in olive oil until soft, but not brown. Add beans, onion, garlic, wine, Worcestershire sauce, and Louisiana hot sauce. After the beans are tender, salt to taste, and cook until done to your taste. Serve over rice. Serves eight.

Asparagus-Tuna Casserole

2 cans (14½ oz. each) asparagus, drained into a cup
2 tbsp. olive oil
2 cups onion
1 large can (12½ oz.) tuna, drained and broken
3 cups grated cheddar cheese
2 eggs
½ cup sauterne
½ cup asparagus juice
lemon pepper seasoning
1 tsp. salt
1 cup fresh, parbroiled mushrooms
Parmesan cheese
1 cup seasoned bread crumbs

Sauté the onions in olive oil. Make one layer each of asparagus, cheese, and mushrooms in your casserole dish. Sprinkle with lemon pepper seasoning. Mix tuna with the sautéed onion. Layer this, along with another layer of cheese, and sprinkle Parmesan and lemon pepper seasoning on the top. Beat eggs, wine, and asparagus juice. Add salt. Pour over all. Sprinkle bread crumbs on top.

Bake at 350° until bread crumbs are brown.

Eggplant Casserole a la Justin

4 qts. chopped eggplant
2 cups chopped onion
1 cup parsley
1 tsp. celery salt
1 tsp. butter-flavored salt
1 tsp. onion powder
1 tsp. garlic powder
1 cup sauterne wine
1 cup tuna
1 cup shrimp
2 cups water
2 tbsp. Worcestershire
2 tsp. Louisiana hot sauce
2 eggs
Progresso bread crumbs
1 cup chopped bell pepper
salt
2 tbsp. olive oil
1 tbsp. soy sauce

Marinate the eggplant in salt water, rinse, and drain. Cook eggplant in a mixture of sauterne, water, Worcestershire, hot sauce, and soy sauce until it can be mashed. Pour it into a colander, saving the juice.

Sauté the onions, bell pepper, and parsley in olive oil until clear or tender. Add onion powder, garlic powder, celery salt, and butter-flavored salt. Combine this mixture, the shrimp, and tuna with the eggplant. Mix well, using a little of the juice that was saved for extra flavor. Beat the eggs and fold in. Place in a casserole dish and top with bread crumbs.

Bake in 350-degree oven 45 minutes to an hour.

Brussels Sprouts au Gratin

olive oil
brussels sprouts, cooked and drained
onion, sliced
1 cup Romano or Parmesan cheese
1 cup grated Swiss cheese
1 cup grated American cheese
1 cup sauterne wine
salt
red pepper

Cover the bottom and the sides of a casserole dish with olive oil. Place in the casserole a layer of brussels sprouts, sliced onion, and three kinds of cheese. Salt and pepper to taste. Repeat the layering until the casserole is full, seasoning each layer. Pour wine over the whole mess.

Bake at 375° for 1 hour or until tender.

Turnip Casserole

10 cups cooked and mashed turnips
1 cup chopped green onion
½ lb. diced bacon
½ cup dried parsley
salt to taste
2 cups seasoned bread crumbs
1 tbsp. soy sauce
½ tsp. hot sauce
½ cup sauterne wine
½ tsp. garlic powder
1 cup grated cheese
1 cup tuna
1 cup chopped clams
4 eggs, beaten

Layer the turnips, cheese, tuna, clams, onions, bacon, and bread crumbs. Make 2 layers.

Beat eggs, and blend in with the rest of the ingredients. Pour this mixture over the layers in the dish. Bake at 350° until brown.

Rhody Macaroni

1 cup macaroni
1 tbsp. butter
4 oz. cheese
4 oz. mushrooms
1 egg, beaten
crackers
salt
pepper

Cook the macaroni 7 minutes, drain under cold water, and set aside. Select a baking pan of 1-quart capacity. Warm and line with 1 tablespoon butter. Put 1/3 of the macaroni in the pan, grate or slice some cheddar cheese over the macaroni, add 1 tablespoon of mushroom pieces and 6 saltines, and cover with milk. Continue adding the same layers until all of the ingredients are used.

Add one beaten egg to the milk and put on the second layer. Top off with a few bits of cheese, which will brown and give a bit of color. Cook, uncovered, in a moderate oven.

NOTE: Be sure that the milk covers the entire surface of this dish before placing it in the oven. Salt and pepper should be used to taste about the middle of the assembly. Quantities of cheese and mushrooms may be used to suit your taste. Cooking time is governed by the depth of the pan, but usually a spoon test should be made after 25 minutes.

Okra Succotash

1 cup chopped onion
1 cup bell pepper (and hot pepper if you have it)
1 tbsp. chopped garlic
3 cups chopped okra
1 can (16 oz.) mashed tomatoes
1 can (16 oz.) creamed corn
salt and pepper to taste

Put all of the ingredients in a big pot and cook until the okra and onions are done. Serve it over rice.

How many will it serve? I don't know. It depends on how many are comin' and how hungry they are!

Eggplant and Cheese

olive oil
bacon drippings
eggplant, sliced
soy sauce
Swiss cheese, grated
Romano or Parmesan cheese, grated
American cheese
salt
red pepper

Salt and pepper the eggplant. Fry the sliced eggplant in a mixture of olive oil and bacon drippings. Drain well after frying.

Layer the eggplant in a heavy platter. Sprinkle soy sauce and Romano and Swiss cheeses on each layer except the top. Place a layer of sliced American cheese on the top. Heat in a warm oven until the cheese melts.

This is good cold and chopped like chocolate candy. It can also be used as an appetizer.

You can look at me an' tol', when I shop on dem grocery store, I should never go dare hungry like I am here, no.

Squash and Shrimp

8 cups chopped squash
3 cups chopped onion
1 cup bell pepper
1 cup dried shrimp
1 big clove garlic, minced
salt
1 cup sauterne wine
red pepper
bread crumbs
Parmesan cheese
1 large banana pepper, chopped (or pickled hot pepper)
3 eggs, beaten well
2 tbsp. olive oil

Put 2 tablespoons olive oil in a large pot. Sauté the onion, hot pepper, and bell pepper until clear. Add the squash, and 1 cup wine. Cook until tender. Stir in the shrimp and garlic, and cook 10 minutes. Beat the eggs and fold into the squash mixture.

Turn into a deep casserole dish. Top with bread crumbs and Parmesan cheese. Bake at 325° for 1 hour or until brown.

Molded Green Beans Almondine

2 pkg. (8 oz. each) softened cream cheese
2 cans (10½ oz. each) condensed chicken broth
1 cup finely chopped parsley
2 tbsp. lemon juice
3 pkg. (10 oz. each) frozen cut green beans, cooked until tender
2 envelopes plain gelatin
1 cup water
¾ cup toasted slivered almonds

Beat cheese until soft; mix in the undiluted chicken broth. Fold in the cooked green beans, parsley, and lemon juice. Soften the gelatin in water in a small saucepan, then stir over low heat until dissolved. Stir into the salad mixture. In a shallow pan, toast almonds at 400° for 5 minutes. Add hot almonds to the salad.

Turn the mixture into a 2½-quart mold and chill until set. Unmold onto plate and garnish with parsley.

Dis lady here is Mrs. Audrey Scivique. She got a fine restaurant down where I live, and dat ain't all. She's a damn good cook, too, you hear?

Pickled Sweet Mirliton

1 pt. raw, sliced mirliton (1/8-1/4 in. thick slices)
1/3 cup vinegar
1/4 cup beet juice
1/3 cup sugar
1/4 tsp. whole allspice
1 stick whole cinnamon
1/16 tsp. whole cloves
1/8 tsp. salt

Combine the vinegar, beet juice, sugar, spices, and salt. Bring to a boil, then simmer 15 minutes. Simmer mirliton five minutes. Pack into hot, sterilized jars. Bring syrup back to a boil and pour over the mirliton. If not enough to cover, add hot vinegar. Seal immediately.

You can do anyt'ing you want to wit' mirliton an' it will taste good. As a matter of fact, mirliton can do mos' anyt'ing but drive a car!

Black-Eyed Pea Jambalaya

1/2 lb. bacon, cut in 1-in. cubes
2 cups black-eyed peas (fresh, frozen, or dried)
1 tsp. salt
1 cup long grain rice

Cook the bacon in 2 quarts of water for about 1 hour. Then add the black-eyed peas. Continue cooking for 30 minutes, or until the peas are almost tender. Add salt and rice and boil about 15 to 18 minutes longer.

Drain the peas and rice thoroughly, and place in a casserole dish in a warm oven for a few minutes until rice is fluffy. Serve with sliced bacon on the top.

Fried Green Tomatoes

olive oil (or shortening)
6 tomatoes, sliced
1/2 cup cornmeal
1/4 cup flour
ground red cayenne pepper
1 tsp. salt

Heat the oil in a frying pan over a high fire. Blend the dry ingredients. Roll the tomatoes in dry ingredients. Fry the tomatoes in hot grease until golden brown on both sides.

Black-Eyed Pea Balls

about 3 cups cooked black-eyed peas, drained
1 cup ground beef
ground cayenne pepper to taste
½ cup finely chopped green onion
salt
2 eggs, well beaten
seasoned bread crumbs
plain flour
cooking oil
1 tbsp. Lea & Perrins

Mix drained peas, meat, and chopped onions well. Salt and pepper to taste. Beat the eggs and Lea & Perrins together thoroughly, and blend into the peas and meat. Add bread crumbs until the mixture is cohesive enough to roll in flour. Make into balls.

Cook in oil heated to 325°. Balls will float when done.

Cacusca Squash Casserole

1 cup chopped onion
8 cups sliced cacusca squash
½ cup chopped bell pepper
2 cloves garlic, chopped
1 tbsp. soy sauce
¼ tsp. bitters (Peychaud or Angostura)
1 tsp. Louisiana hot sauce
1 cup sauterne wine
1 cup diced bacon
2 cups diced shrimp
Pam
seasoned bread crumbs

Spray a casserole dish with Pam. Cook all of the ingredients together (except the bread crumbs) until the squash is tender. Put them in the casserole. Sprinkle seasoned bread crumbs on the top. Bake at 325° for 30 to 45 minutes.

Sautéed Mushrooms

3 lbs. fresh mushrooms
2 tbsp. olive oil
1 stick margarine
1½ cups sauterne wine
2 tbsp. soy sauce
½ tsp. cayenne pepper
1 tbsp. lime or lemon juice
1½ tsp. salt
½ tsp. garlic powder

Soak mushrooms in salt water, wash, and then soak them in fresh water. Drain. Put 2 tablespoons olive oil in a skillet. Add all the other ingredients and sauté until the mushrooms are tender.

And you talk about good! They'll give you indigestion, but they're mighty fine!

Cacusca Stew

1 medium cacusca squash, cut up
1 large bell pepper, chopped
3 leaves celery, chopped
2 large onions, chopped
1 bunch green onions, chopped
2 cloves garlic, chopped
½ lb. bacon, cut into pieces
4 cups diced potatoes
1 can Ro Tel
1 can (16 oz.) tomatoes
2 cans (8 oz. each) tomato sauce
2 cups sauterne wine
1 lb. fresh mushrooms
1½ tbsp. salt
2 tbsp. soy sauce
water to cover well

Make a roux first if you want to. I like it better that way. Mix all the ingredients together any damned way you want to and bring to a boil. Simmer for 3 hours.

Leftovers

Leftover Spaghetti Casserole I

Whenever you cook spaghetti, you can put anything you want in the leftovers to make a casserole.

spaghetti
olive oil
American cheese, grated
Swiss cheese, grated
Romano cheese, grated
dried parsley
6 eggs
butter-flavored salt
¼ tsp. bitters (Peychaud or Angostura)
1 tbsp. Lea & Perrins (or soy sauce)
1 tsp. Louisiana hot sauce (or ½ tsp. Tabasco)
2 cups sauterne wine
bacon, sliced

Grease a casserole dish with the olive oil. Put a layer of leftover spaghetti and a layer of three cheeses, and sprinkle some dried parsley on top.

Put all of the flavors in the wine, and beat together with the eggs. Pour all over the whole thing. Take sliced bacon and strip it on the top. Cook at 325° until the bacon is done.

Dat's what you call a "musgo" casserole. It mus' go down!

Leftover Spaghetti Casserole II

Use the same ingredients as Leftover Spaghetti Casserole I, and add 2 pounds peeled shrimp. Make two layers, one with spaghetti and one with shrimp and cheese. Put all of the flavors in the wine, and mix with the eggs. Pour over the layers. Add seasoned bread crumbs on the top of this one. Cook at 325° until bacon is done. For both, Ro Tel may be used instead of wine.

Ham Kabobs With Rice Salad

- 1 cup uncooked brown rice
- 2 cups water
- 1 tsp. salt
- ¼ cup bottled clear French dressing
- 1 tbsp. honey
- ½ cup finely diced celery
- 2 tbsp. sliced green onion (or scallions)
- 2 tbsp. canned pimento, chopped
- 2 tbsp. mayonnaise
- crisp lettuce leaves
- 32 cubes (1 in. each) leftover ham
- 24 honeydew melon balls
- 8 maraschino cherries (optional)

In a heavy 1½-quart saucepan, combine rice, water, and salt. Place over moderately high heat (about 275°) and bring to a full boil. Reduce heat to moderately low (about 225°) and cover pan tightly. Cook 40 to 45 minutes, or until the rice is tender and all of the liquid is absorbed.

Turn the rice into a large bowl and stir in French dressing and honey. Cover and chill in the refrigerator about 1 hour. When the rice is cold, add the celery, onions, pimento, and mayonnaise.

Spoon equal amounts of the rice salad onto each of four lettuce-lined plates. On each of eight wooden skewers, arrange alternately four ham cubes and three melon balls. End with a cherry if desired. Place two kabobs on each plate with the salad. Makes four servings.

The law don' got me, I got him. An' we been talkin' about cookin' an' he's a damn good cook. His name is C. J. "J. J." Berthelot. (C. J. is his fron' name.) An' like I tol' you, he a damn good cook, I garontee!

Turkey Hash

- ½ cup flour
- 1½ tbsp. bacon drippings (or cooking oil)
- 3 cups chopped onion
- 2 cups chopped celery
- 1 cup chopped bell or sweet pepper
- 2 cups chopped green onion (or shallots)
- 1 cup chopped parsley
- 1 tbsp. chopped garlic
- ½ large lemon, chopped
- ½ tsp. dried mint
- 3 tbsp. Worcestershire
- 2 tsp. Louisiana hot sauce (or 1 tsp. Tabasco)
- 1 cup sauterne wine
- ¼ tsp. bitters (Peychaud or Angostura)
- salt
- 1 cup chopped carrots
- 6 cups leftover turkey (at least)
- water
- 3 cups chopped Irish potatoes

Make a roux with the flour and bacon drippings. Add chopped onion, celery, and bell pepper after the roux is browned. Simmer until the vegetables are clear or tender. Stir in the chopped parsley, green onion, and garlic and simmer until tender.

Add lemon, dried mint, bitters, Worcestershire sauce, hot sauce, carrots, potatoes, and a little water. Simmer for 15 minutes. Pour the mixture into a baking pan. Add the turkey, wine, and enough water to not quite cover. Salt to taste. Bake in a 325- to 350-degree oven until brown and not quite dry.

You can use the same ingredients to make hash out of any kind of roast (beef, pork, venison). But for these, add 1 teaspoon dried mint. The mint brings out the flavor of the meat.

After you make dis turkey hash, you can't look another turkey in the face 'til nex' Thanksgiving. Dat's for true, I garontee!

Leftover Macaroni and Cheese

Slice leftover macaroni in 1-inch slices. Put on a bed of lettuce. Top with mayonnaise and paprika and have a nice salad.

Ham Soufflé

¼ cup butter (or margarine)
¼ cup finely chopped, peeled onion
¼ cup flour
1 cup milk
½ cup shredded sharp cheddar cheese
½ tsp. Worcestershire
¼ tsp. salt
¼ tsp. dry mustard
5 eggs, at room temperature (separate yolks and whites)
1 tbsp. chopped, fresh parsley
1½ cups finely diced or chopped leftover baked ham

Heat oven to 350°. In a small saucepan over moderate heat (about 250°), melt the butter. Add the onion and cook until tender. Quickly stir in the flour and blend until smooth. (A wire whip is helpful.) Heat until the flour mixture is bubbly. Remove the pan from the heat and gradually stir in milk. Return the mixture to heat and bring to a boil, stirring constantly.

Add cheese, Worcestershire, salt, and mustard; cook, stirring constantly, until cheese melts. Remove the pan from the heat.

In a large bowl, slightly beat the egg yolks. Gradually stir the hot cheese mixture into the yolks; blend smooth. Stir in parsley and ham. Beat the egg whites until stiff, but not dry. Fold the egg whites into the ham mixture. Turn the mixture into an ungreased 2-quart soufflé dish.

Bake 45 minutes, or until a knife inserted in the center comes out clean. Serve immediately. Makes four to six servings.

Lamb Salad

- 1½ cups diced leftover roast lamb
- 2 tbsp. bottled clear French dressing
- 1 tbsp. lemon juice
- ½ cup diced celery
- ¼ cup chopped, seeded green pepper
- 1 tbsp. chopped, peeled onion
- 1 tbsp. drained capers
- 1 tbsp. canned pimento, chopped
- ¼ cup mayonnaise
- 2 tbsp. crumbled blue cheese
- ¼ tsp. dried mint
- ¼ tsp. garlic salt
- dash of Tabasco
- crisp lettuce leaves
- fresh parsley sprigs

In a bowl, combine lamb, French dressing, and lemon juice. Add celery, green pepper, onion, pimento, and capers to the lamb mixture. Set aside while preparing remaining ingredients. Stir occasionally.

In a small bowl, blend together the mayonnaise, cheese, mint, garlic salt, and Tabasco. Stir into the lamb mixture. Spoon equal amounts of the salad onto two or three lettuce-lined plates. Garnish with parsley. Makes two to three servings.

Ham Salad Stuffed Tomatoes

- 1½ cups finely diced leftover baked ham
- ½ cup finely diced celery
- ¼ cup chopped pecans
- 2 tbsp. chopped, pimento-stuffed olives
- ¼ cup mayonnaise
- 1 tbsp. finely chopped, peeled onion
- 1 tbsp. chili sauce
- 4 medium-sized tomatoes
- crisp lettuce leaves
- fresh parsley sprigs

Mix together the ham, celery, pecans, olives, and onion in a large bowl. Stir in the mayonnaise and chili sauce.

Placing the stem end down on a board, cut each tomato about two-thirds of the way down into 8 wedges. Gently push wedges open to allow space for stuffing. Place each tomato on a lettuce-lined salad plate and stuff with equal amounts of the ham salad. Garnish plates with parsley. Makes four servings.

You see dat bottle I got on my hand? Dat is at *least* fo' hundred an' forty fo' yards of red pepper hell, I garontee!

Sauces, Salad Dressings, and Jellies

Remoulade Sauce a la Justin

1 gal. mayonnaise
20 oz. Dijon mustard
20 oz. Durkee's dressing
16 oz. horseradish
2 tsp. salt
6 oz. Louisiana hot sauce
½ small bottle of Lea & Perrins
1 tsp. cayenne pepper
1 tsp. celery salt

Thoroughly mix all of the ingredients together. Make a lot and keep it. The sauce will keep indefinitely. And it's delicious!

Cajunized Chinese Sauce

hot peppers, in strips
bell peppers, in strips
1 tsp. lemon pepper seasoning
olive oil
1 tbsp. soy sauce
½ cup sauterne wine
1 tsp. Lea & Perrins
½ tsp. onion powder
¼ tsp. garlic powder
½ tsp. bitters (Peychaud or Angostura)

Mix the Lea & Perrins, onion powder, garlic powder, soy sauce, lemon pepper, bitters, and wine. Spread over any type meat, along with the vegetables. Grease the pan you are cooking the meat in with olive oil, and pour the mixture over the whole doggone thing. Bake at 325° to 350° until your meat is done.

Apple Butter

12 large cooking apples
1 qt. water
5 cups sugar (or more)
6 cups apple cider
2 tsp. cinnamon
2 tsp. ground cloves
1 tsp. allspice
1 pt. sauterne wine

Wash, quarter, and core apples. Cook in water and wine until soft, about 10 minutes. (If using a blender to mash cooked apples, peel apples before cooking.) Force the mixture through a sieve or food mill, discarding the skins. Add half as much sugar as you have pulp.

In a large saucepan, heat cider to boiling. Add the apple mixture and cook over medium heat until 1 teaspoon of the apple mixture dropped onto a cold plate will hold its shape. Stir the mixture often to prevent sticking, adding spices as it thickens.

Apple Butter thickens when chilled. The mixture should be thick enough to spread. Makes about four pints.

Chow Chow

1 gal. green tomatoes
1 head cabbage
4 large onions
½ cup salt
1 tsp. allspice
1 tsp. cloves
1 tsp. cinnamon
1 cup sugar
2 to 3 cloves garlic, chopped fine
1 qt. vinegar
2 to 3 hot green peppers

Chop the tomatoes and place in a crock pot or large enamel bowl. Add ½ cup salt and stir. Let it sit overnight.

The next day, soak tomatoes, cabbage, and onion all together for two hours. Drain off the juice. Add allspice, cinnamon, cloves, sugar, garlic, and hot peppers. Pour over enough vinegar to boil (about 1 quart). Cook until the tomatoes are tender.

Place the mixture in jars while hot and seal. (Taste for salt. If too salty, rinse before you place in jars.)

Tasty Black-Eyed Pea Dip

½ lb. dried black-eyed peas
1 cup water
1 cup sauterne wine
1¼ tsp. salt
⅓ cup diced lean ham
1 can (4 oz.) green chiles
½ tsp. red food coloring
½ cup chopped onion
1 cup tomato juice
⅛ tsp. garlic powder
½ jar (8 oz.) processed cheese spread
¼ tsp. hot pepper sauce

Wash peas; cover with water and allow to soak overnight.

The next morning, drain the peas and cover with one cup water and 1 cup sauterne. Put all of this in a heavy saucepan and bring to a boil. Lower the temperature, cover the pan, and simmer for 30 minutes. Add salt and ham, and simmer 25 to 30 minutes longer; add red food coloring. Drain peas, reserving liquid.

Drain and chop the chiles, reserving 2 tablespoons liquid. Place the peas, chiles, reserved juice from chiles, tomato juice, onion, and garlic powder in a blender container; blend to make a puree. (If a blender is not available, put mixture through a food mill.) Add a small amount of liquid reserved from peas, if needed, to obtain desired consistency.

Spoon the mixture into the top of a double boiler; add the cheese spread and pepper sauce. Cook over medium heat until the cheese melts. Serve warm with crackers or corn chips. Makes ten to twelve servings.

Slaw Dressing

½ cup sugar
¼ cup vinegar
1 tsp. dry mustard
1 tsp. salt
½ tsp. red pepper
1 cup olive oil
1 tsp. celery seed
1 tbsp. lemon juice
1 cup mayonnaise

Cook the sugar, vinegar, mustard, salt, and red pepper for 15 to 20 minutes. Remove from fire and let cool. Add mayonnaise. Beat in the oil slowly. Add celery seed, lemon juice, and more salt (if necessary), and mix thoroughly.

I wanna tol' you, dat devilish gleam what I got in ma eye is to let you know dat ain't catsup I'm pourin' on dat meat, no. Dat's ground red cayenne pepper, an' ooh whee! It's got some seasoning on dat. Not too hot, jus' rat.

Gina's Relish

1 doz. green bell peppers
1 doz. red bell peppers
10 medium onions
3 cups vinegar
1 tsp. salt
1 tsp. celery salt
2 cups sugar
1 tbsp. ground cloves

Grind the peppers and onions. Put in a colander; pour boiling water over, stirring well. Let drain. Put the mixture in a pot and again pour boiling water over. Let it stand 10 minutes, then drain well.

Mix the vinegar, salt, celery salt, sugar, and cloves. Add to the relish and boil for 20 to 25 minutes.

Two bushels of peppers make 8 bushels cooked. Use approximately 2 quarts of vinegar, 20 pounds of onions, and 20 pounds of sugar to make 47 pints.

Bordelaise Sauce a la Sara

¼ lb. oleo (or butter)
½ tsp. finely chopped garlic
1 tbsp. parsley
1 tbsp. sauterne wine
1 tbsp. soy sauce
2 tbsp. lemon juice
½ tsp. Louisiana hot sauce (or ¼ tsp. Tabasco)
½ cup chopped mushrooms

Sauté the mushrooms and parsley in butter or oleo. Add the hot sauce, soy sauce, lemon juice, and garlic. Finish with sauterne wine. Cook for 15 to 20 minutes. Serve over steak or chops.

Mermaid Sauce

1 pt. salad dressing
1 tsp. chopped garlic
½ cup sauterne wine
1 tsp. salt
2 tsp. Louisiana hot sauce (or 1 tsp. Tabasco)
2 tsp. Lea & Perrins
2 tsp. honey

Mix all of the ingredients together. Use over a green salad.

Pepper Jelly

1 pt. apple jelly
1 tbsp. finely chopped bell pepper
½ tsp. chopped hot pepper

Over low heat, slowly melt one pint of apple jelly. To the melted jelly, add the bell pepper and hot pepper. Pour the mixture back into the jar and cover.

For color, use combined red and green pepper. To make jelly more spicy, use more pepper to taste.

Honey Dressing

¼ cup sugar
1 tsp. dry mustard
1 tsp. paprika
1 tsp. celery seed
1 tsp. salt
1/3 cup vinegar
1/3 cup honey
1 tbsp. lemon juice
onion juice, if desired
1 cup salad oil

In a small mixing bowl, beat all of the ingredients except the oil. Add the oil slowly, beating constantly.

This dressing is good for the same as slaw dressing or for fruit salads.

If you leave the salad oil out, this can also be used as a sweet-and-sour sauce.

Breads, Biscuits, and Dumplings

Sourdough Biscuits

1 pkg. yeast
1 cup warm water
2 cups buttermilk
½ cup sugar
4 tsp. baking powder
½ cup cooking oil
1 tsp. salt
¼ tsp. soda
5 cups flour (maybe more)

Dissolve yeast in water. Mix together thoroughly with all of the ingredients except flour. Add 5 or more cups of flour and mix well.

Put the dough in a covered bowl in the refrigerator for 12 hours or more before using. When ready to bake, roll out the dough and pinch off biscuits. Bake in a greased pan at 450° until golden brown.

Brunch Yam Bread

1 can (1-lb. size) Louisiana yams in orange-pineapple sauce
¾ cup sauce from yams
2 eggs
1 tbsp. lemon juice
1 tsp. grated lemon rind
2½ cups biscuit mix
1 tsp. cinnamon
½ tsp. nutmeg
¼ tsp. allspice
¼ cup milk

Place the yams and sauce in a mixing bowl and mash well. Stir in lemon juice and rind; beat in eggs. Add the biscuit mix and spices and beat well. Stir in milk.

Spoon the batter into a greased loaf pan (9-inch x 5-inch x 3-inch), and bake in a preheated 350-degree oven 55 to 65 minutes. Turn out on a rack to cool. Slice and serve warm with butter.

Murphy Brown, Walter Guitreau, me, an' Jean Pierre Malbrough got a good discuss goin' on here. You can tol' dat. But I can't garontee it's about cookin', no.

Cornbread Dressing

1 loaf toasted cornbread
6 cups finely chopped celery
6 cups finely chopped onion
6 raw eggs, well beaten
12 slices toast, crumbled
1 tsp. sage
salt and pepper to taste
10 cups hot stock (chicken or turkey)
enough hot water to make heavy mixture

Bake the cornbread until brown. (See my recipe.) Stir all of the ingredients together with the cornbread. Pour into a baking pan.

Bake at 325° for approximately one hour and a half, or until brown. You can check dis like a cake.

Maxine's French Bread

1 qt. warm water
2 oz. yeast (3 pkg.)
1 oz. salt (3 tsp.)
2 tsp. lard
6 tbsp. sugar
11 cups flour

Mix all of the ingredients in the water, adding the flour last. Let the dough rise 1 hour. Knead and mold, and let stand another ½ hour. Bake in a 400-degree oven until brown.

Potato Klosse

2 lbs. boiled potatoes
1½ slices toasted bread, crumbled
1 pat of butter
2 eggs, beaten
2 to 3 tbsp. flour (or more)
1 tbsp. finely chopped onion
1 tbsp. finely chopped parsley
salt
3 qts. salted, boiling water

Either mash or grate the potatoes. Simmer the onions, parsley, and butter, and mix well with the potatoes and flour. Add the eggs and bread crumbs. Make smooth round balls. (Flour your hands before making balls.) Place the potato balls in the boiling water and simmer for 8 to 10 minutes.

Martha's Beer Biscuits

2 cups Bisquick
½ cup finely chopped green onion
2 tbsp. shortening
½ cup shredded cheddar cheese
beer

Mix together the Bisquick, onion, and cheese. Cut the shortening into the mixture, and add enough beer to make the dough slightly stiff. Turn out onto a Bisquick-covered board. Knead a few times and cut into individual biscuits. Bake at 450° until browned.

Refrigerator Biscuits

5 cups self-rising flour
1 tsp. soda
1 cup Crisco
2 cups buttermilk
¼ cup warm water
1 pkg. dry yeast

Dissolve the yeast in warm water and set aside. Mix the other ingredients and add to the yeast mixture. Knead on a floured board until smooth.

You can make some biscuits now and store the rest of the mixture in a plastic bag in the refrigerator. No rising is required before baking. Bake as many as you want when you want them. The longer the mixture stays in the refrigerator, the better the biscuit. Bake at 400° until done. Make very small biscuits because they double in size while baking.

Dumplings for Chicken or Anything Else

2 cups all-purpose flour
3 tsp. baking powder
¾ tsp. salt
2 tbsp. bacon drippings
1 cup (scant) cold bouillon or meat stock

Sift together the flour, salt, and the baking powder. Cut in the bacon drippings. Moisten with broth to make a drop batter. Drop the dumplings by teaspoonfuls into boiling soup. Cover and steam for 12 minutes.

Biscuits

2 cups all-purpose flour
3 tsp. baking powder
½ tsp. salt
1¼ cups buttermilk
½ tsp. baking soda
2 tbsp. shortening

Sift the dry ingredients together. Blend in the shortening and buttermilk and mix well.

Roll the biscuits out on waxed paper covered with flour. Cut and place in a greased pan. Bake in a 475-degree oven for about 15 minutes.

Cornpone

1 cup yellow cornmeal (home ground if possible)
¾ cup plain flour
1 tsp. salt
2 tsp. baking powder
½ tsp. onion powder
¼ tsp. garlic powder
2 eggs
1 cup milk (maybe more)

Mix the dry ingredients. Add some of the milk until you can work the batter. Beat the eggs and add to the batter. Make batter thin enough to fry, just like you would pancakes. Remember, if you want thick cornpone cakes, you must have thick batter.

These are good, and something else about them. They can be fixed real quick, so you can have cornpone with greens or whatever you want to have it with. Also, too, be sure an' butter 'em real good.

Cornbread

1½ cups yellow cornmeal
1 cup flour
3 tsp. baking powder
2 eggs
1 cup milk
1 tsp. salt
2 tbsp. shortening

Heat the shortening in a skillet. Mix the dry ingredients well. Beat the eggs, and blend in with dry ingredients. Add milk to reach desired consistency (not too runny). Pour the shortening from the hot skillet into the batter and beat real good.

Bake in a preheated 350-degree oven until brown. When brown, take the cornbread out of the oven and flip it over to sweat it. If you don't, it will mildew. Turn the oven off. Place the cornbread back in the skillet and keep warm in the oven.

Margie Stolz' German Dumplings

2 eggs
½ cup sweet milk
1½ cups flour
¼ tsp. salt
½ tsp. baking powder

Beat the eggs; add milk. Sift the flour, salt, and baking powder. Stir this into the egg mixture and beat well, until the dough becomes smooth and elastic. Let the dough rest for about 20 minutes.

With a greased spoon, pinch off a small spoonful of dough and drop into simmering chicken gravy or broth. As you drop dumplings into the gravy, dip the spoon into the liquid to keep it greased for easier handling. Cook slowly for 15 to 20 minutes, or until the dumplings are tender.

If the dumplings are to be served with greens, vegetables, or other dishes, drop them into 3 quarts of boiling water, add 1 teaspoon salt, and simmer until tender. Drain and serve as desired.

Mexican Cornbread

1 cup flour
1½ cups cornmeal
3 tsp. baking powder
1 tsp. salt
½ tsp. soda
1 tsp. sugar
1 can Mexicorn
½ cup bacon drippings
2 eggs
1 cup grated cheese
2 jalapeno peppers, chopped
2 tbsp. chopped bell pepper
1 cup sour cream or buttermilk

Mix all of the ingredients together except the cheese. Pour half of the mixture into a greased hot skillet. Sprinkle half of the cheese on the top, then add the rest of the mixture and the remaining cheese. Bake at 350° for 45 minutes.

Desserts

Pumpkin Pie With Praline Topping a la Maxine

9-in. unbaked pie shell
2 eggs
1 can (1 lb.) pumpkin
¾ cup firmly packed light brown sugar
½ tsp. salt
1½ tsp. pumpkin pie spice
1 tall can evaporated milk (1 ⅔ cups)
Praline Topping (See recipe.)

In a medium-sized mixing bowl, beat the eggs slightly. Stir in pumpkin, brown sugar, salt, spice, and evaporated milk, mixing well. Pour most of the filling into the pastry shell, then place the pie on the oven rack. Pour in the rest of the filling. (This helps to keep from spilling.)

Bake in a preheated hot oven (400°) for 15 minutes; turn oven temperature down to moderate (350°) and continue baking 45 minutes longer, or until the filling is done when tested. Cool pie slightly, then refrigerate until serving time.

When ready to serve, make Praline Topping, and sprinkle evenly over pie. Place the pie under broiler heat until the topping is bubbly (about 1 minute) watching carefully so that the mixture does not burn. Serve at once. Makes one 9-inch pie.

PRALINE TOPPING

2 tbsp. margarine
½ cup firmly packed light brown sugar
⅓ cup chopped pecans (peanuts or walnuts may be used instead)

In a small saucepan, melt the margarine. Remove from heat. Stir in brown sugar and pecans. Pour over Pumpkin Pie.

Don' start dat foolishment wit' me. Dat's the one I want, not the one you got in your hand over dare. Can't you see where I'm pointin', where ma finger's at rat on it dare, hanh?

Shoo-Fly Pie

¾ cup unsifted flour
½ tsp. cinnamon
⅛ tsp. ground nutmeg
⅛ tsp. ground cloves
½ cup sugar
½ tsp. salt
2 tbsp. butter (or shortening)
1½ tsp. baking soda
¾ cup boiling water
½ cup light molasses
1 egg, well beaten
pastry for a 9-in. pie

In a medium bowl, combine flour, cinnamon, nutmeg, and cloves. Add sugar and salt. Cut in the butter with a pastry knife or with 2 knives until the mixture resembles coarse meal. Dissolve baking soda in boiling water. Add molasses and egg and blend well.

Line a 9-inch pie plate with pastry; shape edges. Pour half of the liquid into the pastry shell. Add ¼ of the flour mixture and stir gently. Pour in the rest of the liquid and top evenly with the remaining flour mixture.

Bake at 400° for 10 minutes. Reduce heat to 325° and bake until the pie is set and the crust is golden (about 25 minutes).

Fruitcake Cookies

1 stick of butter
2 lbs. candied cherries
2 lbs. candied pineapple
2 lbs. mixed fruits
2 tsp. soda
3 tbsp. sweet milk
6 cups pecans
4 eggs
1 cup claret wine
1 tsp. each cinnamon, cloves, allspice, nutmeg, and rum extract
1½ cups packed dark brown sugar
3 cups flour

Cream butter and sugar. Add 1 egg at a time and beat; add wine and milk and beat well. Sift the dry ingredients and add. Sprinkle fruits and pecans with ½ cup flour and add them to the mixture.

Drop by spoonfuls on a greased tin. Bake in a 300-degree oven for 15 to 20 minutes. Makes 200 cookies. Store in a tin can to be frozen.

Pralines

4 cups sugar
4 tbsp. Karo syrup
1 can condensed milk
1 can water
4 to 6 cups pecans
1 tsp. butter
½ tsp. vanilla

Mix all of the ingredients together thoroughly except butter, vanilla, and pecans. Cook over a low fire until the soft boil stage. Remove from heat.

Add butter, vanilla, and pecans. Beat until the mixture holds its shape. Spoon on buttered waxed paper.

Jiffy Gel Sundaes

1 pkg. (3 oz.) black cherry jello
1 qt. vanilla ice cream or pineapple sherbert

Empty the jello into a medium bowl. Add 2/3 cup boiling water and stir until the jello is dissolved. Divide among eight dessert dishes, 1 quart of vanilla ice cream or pineapple sherbert. Spoon hot jello mixture over ice cream. The cherry sauce thickens as it touches the ice cream. Makes eight servings.

Try your own favorite flavors of jello and ice cream for a rainbow of sundae toppings.

Sweet Tooth Dessert

1 small can crushed or chunk pineapple, drained
1 small can mandarin oranges, drained
1 large can cherry pie filling
1 can Eagle Brand sweetened milk
1 carton (9 oz.) Cool Whip

Mix, mix, mix. Keep cool, cool, cool. Top with Cool Whip.

Raisin Supreme a la Justin

6 to 8 cups seedless raisins
1 cup brandy
1 cup Benedictine
½ cup honey
1 tsp. cinnamon
¼ tsp. bitters (Peychaud or Angostura)

Put all of the ingredients in a pan on the stove and bring to a boil (not a rolling boil). Simmer, covered, for 2 hours.

This delicious supreme can be put over ice cream, lemon pie, or even vanilla wafers, for a tasty treat.

Pumpkin-Raisin Loaves

¾ can canned pumpkin
1 egg
1 pkg. (14 oz.) apple-cinnamon muffin mix
⅓ cup water
1 tsp. pumpkin pie spice
½ cup raisins

In a mixing bowl, combine the pumpkin, water, egg, and pumpkin pie spice. Add the muffin mix and raisins; stir just until moistened. Turn into 3 greased 5½-inch x 3-inch x 2-inch loaf pans (or one 9-inch x 5-inch x 3-inch loaf pan).

Bake small loaves in a moderate oven (350°) for 35 to 40 minutes. Bake larger loaf 50 minutes. Turn from the pan and cool on rack.

Drizzle loaves with powdered sugar icing. (Add enough milk to 2 cups sifted powdered sugar to make a pouring consistency.)

Lemon Pie

1 can condensed milk
1 can lemonade (frozen concentrate)
1 large carton Cool Whip
graham cracker pie crust (or vanilla wafers)

Mix all of the ingredients together (except Cool Whip) and pour over a graham cracker crust or vanilla wafers. Top with Cool Whip.

I wanna let you know rat now dat I'm very saincaire about dis cookin' business. I believe it when I say cookin' is not'ing but imagination an' common sense in the proper amounts.

Sweet Potato Surprise Cake

1½ cups oil
2 cups sugar
4 eggs, separated
4 tbsp. hot water
2½ cups sifted cake flour
3 tsp. baking powder
¼ tsp. salt
1 tsp. ground nutmeg
1½ cups grated, raw sweet potatoes
1 cup chopped nuts
1 tsp. vanilla
1 tsp. ground cinnamon

Combine cooking oil and sugar; beat until smooth. Add egg yolks; beat well. Add hot water, then dry ingredients which have been sifted together. Stir in the potatoes, nuts, and vanilla and beat well. Beat the egg whites until stiff and fold into the mixture.

Bake in three greased 8-inch layer cake pans at 350° for 25 to 30 minutes.

ICING:
1 box powdered sugar, sifted
1 pkg. (8 oz.) cream cheese

Blend powdered sugar with the cream cheese. Gradually add a small amount of milk to which lemon or orange juice has been added. Use to ice Sweet Potato Surprise Cake.

Louisiana Pecan Pie

3 eggs
1 cup brown or white sugar
2 cups pecan meats
1 cup corn syrup
9-in. pie crust
1 tsp. vanilla
½ tsp. salt
1 tsp. butter
3 tbsp. flour

Beat the eggs. Add sugar, syrup, butter, flour, salt, vanilla, and pecans. Pour into a pie crust that has been baked for a few minutes (long enough to dry it out). Then bake in a 350-degree oven for about 1 hour or until firm in the middle.

Date and Nut Bread

2 cups apple cider
2 cups chopped and pitted dates
2 cups granulated sugar
$^2/_3$ cup soft butter (or margarine)
2 eggs
3 cups sifted flour
2 tsp. baking soda
$^1/_8$ tsp. salt
1 tsp. vanilla
2 cups chopped nuts

Bring the apple cider to a boil and pour over the dates. Set aside. Cream butter or margarine and sugar together. Add eggs and mix thoroughly. Sift together the flour, soda, and salt and add to the creamed mixture alternately with vanilla and cider-date mixture. Add nuts.

Grease and flour two bread pans and divide dough equally between them. Bake in 275-degree oven for 1 hour and 45 minutes. While still warm, wrap in waxed paper, and then a clean tea towel.

Louisiana Praline, Yam, and Pecan Dessert Casserole

4 medium Louisiana yams, cooked, peeled, and quartered (or two 16-oz. cans)
$^1/_2$ cup firmly packed dark brown sugar
2 eggs
$^1/_3$ cup melted butter (or margarine)
1 tsp. salt
$^1/_2$ cup pecan halves

Mash yams in a large bowl. Beat in eggs, $^1/_4$ cup of the sugar, 2 tablespoons melted butter, and salt. Turn into a 1-quart casserole. Arrange pecan halves on top, sprinkle with the remaining $^1/_4$ cup sugar, and drizzle with the remaining melted butter.

Bake, uncovered, in a 350-degree oven for 20 minutes. Serve warm with orange sauce. Serves six.

Beer Birthday Cake

2 cups brown sugar
1 cup shortening
2 eggs
1 cup chopped nuts
2 cups chopped dates
1 tsp. cinnamon
½ tsp. allspice
½ tsp. ground cloves
2 cups beer (or ale)
3 cups sifted all-purpose flour
2 tsp. baking soda
½ tsp. salt

Cream the sugar and shortening. Stir in the eggs, nuts, dates, and spices. In a separate bowl, sift together the flour, baking soda, and salt; stir in beer. Combine the beer mixture with the creamed mixture and mix until well blended.

Bake in a large tube pan in a moderate oven (350°) for 1 hour and 15 minutes. If desired, ice with whipped cream or a caramel icing.

Sweet Potato Nutty Chewies

3 cups firmly packed, mashed sweet potatoes
2 cups granulated sugar
½ cup sweet milk
5 tbsp. self-rising flour
2 tsp. vanilla
1 cup coconut
1 cup nuts (preferably pecans)
½ stick of butter
dash of salt

Wash and quarter three medium-sized sweet potatoes. Boil until soft, peel, and mash to measure 3 cups. Add sugar, flour, and milk and beat for 1 minute on medium speed. Add salt and vanilla. Take from the mixer and add with a spoon the nuts and coconut. Melt the butter in a 9-inch x 11-inch pan with a depth of 2 inches. Pour the butter into the mixture, then pour it all back into the same pan.

Bake for 30 minutes at 400°. Let cool and cut into squares to serve as an in-between meal delight or as a dessert at mealtime.

Index

Justin Wilson was an internationally acclaimed humorist who hosted six television cooking series. A prolific author, Wilson wrote ***The Justin Wilson Cookbook***, which features many of the traditional recipes that define Cajun cooking. His other Pelican titles range from irresistible cookbooks to stories about Louisiana's Cajun country: ***Justin Wilson's Easy Cookin': 150 Rib-Tickling Recipes for Good Eating, The Justin Wilson Gourmet and Gourmand Cookbook, Justin Wilson Looking Back: A Cajun Cookbook, Justin Wilson's Outdoor Cooking with Inside Help, Justin Wilson's Cajun Fables, Justin Wilson's Cajun Humor,*** and ***More Cajun Humor***. A lifelong resident of Louisiana, Wilson passed away in 2001.